LIVING STONES
ROCKS

SUSAN SAYERS

Illustrated by
Fred Chevalier

Kevin Mayhew

First published in 1998 by
KEVIN MAYHEW LTD
Rattlesden
Bury St Edmunds
Suffolk IP30 0SZ

0 1 2 3 4 5 6 7 8 9

ISBN 1 84003 214 6
Catalogue No. 1500196

The other titles in the *Living Stones* series are

Complete Resource Book	ISBN 1 84003 212 X	Cat. No. 1500194
Prayers of Intercession	ISBN 1 84003 216 2	Cat. No. 1500198
Pebbles	ISBN 1 84003 213 8	Cat. No. 1500195
Boulders	ISBN 1 84003 215 4	Cat. No. 1500197

Cover photographs:
Group of children – courtesy of SuperStock Ltd, London
Background – courtesy of Images Colour Library Ltd, London
Cover design by Jaquetta Sergeant
Edited by Katherine Laidler
Typesetting by Louise Selfe
Printed in Great Britain

FOREWORD

For children of primary school age the sense of belonging to a peer group becomes increasingly important. Their faith development can be fostered in group activities which are fun and challenging. Their growing awareness of the wider world is often linked with a strong sense of justice and social responsibility, and they need to see the Christian perspective in all this.

Rocks encourages the children to begin thinking about the implications of their faith. Their participation in the story-telling and teaching is welcomed.

It would be wise to split the group into two age groups, adapting the suggestions on the worksheets accordingly.

This is something of a DIY kit, supplied with plenty of openings to meet your own parish needs and the needs of the children, and to spark off your own imaginative ideas. It is based on the belief that children are as much a part of the Church as adults, and that there is great value in sharing the same teaching each Sunday whatever our age. This book follows the weekly readings of the Revised Common Lectionary (Principal Service) for Year A of the three-year cycle, so that the whole church will have that common experience.

Rocks includes a series of weekly activity sheets. These may be copied without further permission or charge for non-commercial use. They can be used as they stand, or you can select the material you want. Copy them for the children to take home, use them in church, put them in the magazine or news sheet, distribute them at clubs or Bible study groups, or use them in conjunction with your learning programme. They are 'working sheets' rather than 'work sheets' as they often include instructions for making and doing rather than being complete in themselves. Children will need their leaders to have planned ahead for the resources needed.

When planning for children's work it is advisable to read through the Bible passages prayerfully. You are then in a better position to see how the programme relates to the readings, and also to supplement and vary the programme as a result of your own insights and the specific needs of your group.

The children are encouraged to pray during the week, using the suggestions on their sheet. These can be built into a collection of prayers and made into a personal prayer book.

A few general ideas about story-telling:

- Tell the story from the viewpoint of a character in the situation. To create the time-machine effect, avoid eye contact as you slowly put on the appropriate cloth or cloak, and then make eye contact as you greet the children in character.

- Have an object with you which leads into the story – a water jug, or a lunch box, for instance.

- Walk the whole group through the story, so that they are physically moving from one place to another; and use all kinds of places, such as broom cupboards, under the stairs, outside under the trees, and so on.

- Collect some carpet tiles – blue and green – so that at story time the children can sit round the edge of this and help you place on the cut-outs for the story.

You may find it useful to keep a record of what you actually do each week, as well as build up a store of the resources you use, because this will obviously help to make future activities easier to prepare.

It is my hope that this book will not only stimulate ideas and enable a varied programme of children's work to take place, but most of all it will encourage us all, whatever our age, as we make the journey of faith together.

SUSAN SAYERS

ACKNOWLEDGEMENT

The publishers wish to express their gratitude to Kingsway's Thankyou Music, PO Box 75, Eastbourne, East Sussex, BN23 6NW for permission to include the chorus from *You laid aside your majesty* by Noel Richards © 1985 (Palm Sunday).

CONTENTS

ORDINARY TIME

This book is dedicated to my family and friends,
whose encouraging support has been wonderful,
and to all those whose good ideas are included here for others to share.

RECOMMENDED
BIBLES

It is often a good idea to look at a passage in several different versions before deciding which to use for a particular occasion.

As far as children are concerned, separate Bible stories, such as those published by Palm Tree Press and Lion, are a good introduction for the very young. Once children are reading, a very helpful version is the *International Children's Bible* (New Century version) published by Word Publishing. Here children have a translation based on experienced scholarship, using language structure suitable for young readers, with short sentences and appropriate vocabulary. There is a helpful dictionary, and clear maps and pictures are provided.

ADVENT

FIRST SUNDAY OF ADVENT

Thought for the day

We are to wake up and make sure we stay ready for the second coming.

Readings

Isaiah 2:1-5
Psalm 122
Romans 13:11-14
Matthew 24:36-44

Aim

To look at the importance of watching and listening in readiness.

Starter

Give half the children a team band, and designate one leader from each group. Mix everyone up together, put on a praise tape and dance or move around to it. Everyone has to do whatever their team leader is doing, changing whenever they change. They will have to concentrate, as people around them will be doing something different.

Teaching

Talk about the way they were very watchful and alert during the dancing, so that they picked up on what their team was doing. We have to be watchful in life as well.

Explain that today is the first Sunday in Advent, and Advent means 'coming'. We are getting ready for Jesus' coming, both remembering him being born at Christmas, and also getting ready for when he comes again in glory. To be ready we need to be watchful and alert. As Christians we will sometimes find that we are living a different way from those around us (like we did in the dancing), but that is because we are following our leader, Jesus, and living his way. That's the best way for us, and the only way to make sure we are ready and don't miss any important instructions, even though it may mean living differently from other people sometimes.

When Jesus had been walking around on earth, teaching, healing and listening to people, he told them a little bit about what would happen at the end of time, so that they, and those who came after them, would be ready for it.

Look together at the Gospel for today, displaying these signs or pictures as you go along:

Praying

Lord, help us to see
the signs of your love today
in the world around us
and in the people we meet.
Train us to be ready to see you
and recognise you
when you come in glory. Amen.

Activities

Have some magnifying glasses so that the children can focus on things and see them in more detail. They can draw what they see on the sheet. There are also some things to look out for which show God at work. The first of the Advent candles will also be lit today, and the children can make the Advent calendar shown on the sheet.

SECOND SUNDAY OF ADVENT

Thought for the day

Get the road ready for the Lord!

Readings

Isaiah 11:1-10
Psalm 72:1-7, 18-19
Romans 15:4-13
Matthew 3:1-12

Aim

To learn about John the Baptist and his message.

Starter

Provide each child with a cardboard tube and some pieces of newspaper. They screw up the newspaper and jam it into the tube. Now ask them to look through their tubes at each other, and they will find that they can't unless they pull out the newspaper which is blocking the view.

Teaching

Point out what a waste of time it was screwing up newspaper and blocking the tubes because that stopped us being able to see through them! Today we are going to look at the way our lives sometimes need unblocking so that God's love can get through to us better.

Tell the story of John the Baptist in the form of an interview with him and one of the leaders. Whoever is being John the Baptist could dress up. Arrange the chairs like a chat show and have John coming in and taking charge, starting to interview the leader. The leader answers a few questions and then says something like: 'Hang on, John, the children know all about me already. It's you they want to meet!' Then interview John, asking about his mother and father, his cousin, his time spent in the desert, and his message to the people. John must sound excited about his message, and the need for people to be ready for the kingdom of God. Ask who came to listen to his teaching, and ask why John got angry with the Pharisees and Sadducees. Like a good interviewer, repeat the important answers to make sure the children have picked them up. Finally thank John for coming and all the children can say goodbye to him.

Praying

Lord God,
help us to get ourselves ready
to welcome you
into our lives. Amen.

Activities

Prepare beforehand a large piece of paper with the sky, desert background, and the River Jordan already drawn. While a couple of children paint in these areas (use sponges which cover the space more quickly than brushes), the other children draw, colour and cut out people coming to listen to John the Baptist. John himself will also be needed. The crowds can be stuck on to the picture. There are some outlines of people on the worksheet for the children to copy or use if you prefer.

The second Advent candle is lit today.

Notes

J	O	H	N	T	H	S	S	W	B
L	O	C	U	S	T	S	O	M	A
I	T	S	P	C	A	C	R	H	P
M	K	S	D	E	S	E	R	T	T
H	I	G	O	D	Y	Y	N	I	
O	N	N	Y	G	J	B	O	A	S
N	G	S	D	S	H	U	G	E	T
E	D	C	A	M	E	L	D	D	N
Y	O	O	E	X	E	J	F	E	O
K	M	G	R	I	V	E	R	E	A

JOHN the **BAPTIST** started preaching in the **DESERT** of **JUDEA**. He wore clothes of **CAMEL** hair and ate **LOCUSTS** and **HONEY**. John told the people '**GET READY** as the **KINGDOM** of **GOD** will soon be here!' The people told God how **SORRY** they were for their **SINS** and John washed them in the **RIVER** as a sign that the lives were made clean.

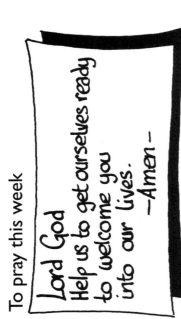

To pray this week

Lord God
Help us to get ourselves ready
to welcome you
into our lives.
—Amen—

You can colour these people, cut them out, and stick them on the big picture. They have all come to hear John the Baptist.

THIRD SUNDAY OF ADVENT

Thought for the day

Great expectations. Jesus fulfils the great statements of prophecy.

Readings

Isaiah 35:1-10
Psalm 146:5-10 or Canticle: Magnificat
James 5:7-10
Matthew 11:2-11

Aim

For the children to learn to expect and allow God to be himself.

Starter

Sit in a circle. In turn each person goes into the middle and says who they are in a special way. (Or they can go in pairs or threes.) They might dance it, score a pretend goal with it, shout it, sing it, or whisper it, drive or bounce it. We're all different and can enjoy one another's different characters.

Teaching

Sit John the Baptist in prison with his back to everyone. He is discreetly blowing bubbles. The story teller explains that he is thinking as he sits in the prison. Can they see his thought bubbles? Have some of his thoughts written on thought-bubble shapes of card, and have them held up over his head in turn as they are mentioned. For example:

- 'Can Jesus be the one we're waiting for?'
- 'He's making friends with sinners instead of judging them!'
- 'He isn't as strict as I expected.'
- 'Jesus isn't behaving the way I thought he would.'

Now get some of John's friends to visit him, so John can ask them to go to Jesus and find out if he really is the Messiah. The friends agree and walk over to Jesus who is healing a small group of people and chatting to them. They ask their question: 'Are you God's Messiah, the one we're waiting to come and save us, or not?'

At this point ask the children what they think Jesus might say. Then go back to the action, to find out what he actually said: 'Look at what I'm doing.' The people around him say what Jesus has done for them: one was blind and can now see, one was deaf and can now hear, one was lame and can now run and jump, and some have been cheered up by being told how much God loves them.

Hold up a large question mark shape. From the evidence, is Jesus the promised Saviour? Put down the question mark and show a large exclamation mark instead. Yes, he is!

Praying

Lord,
help me
to recognise you today. Amen.

Activities

The sheet enables them to take John the Baptist's question, and link it with Jesus' answer. You will need a stapler and the younger children will need help with the cutting out. For some the tricky cutting could be done beforehand.

Notes

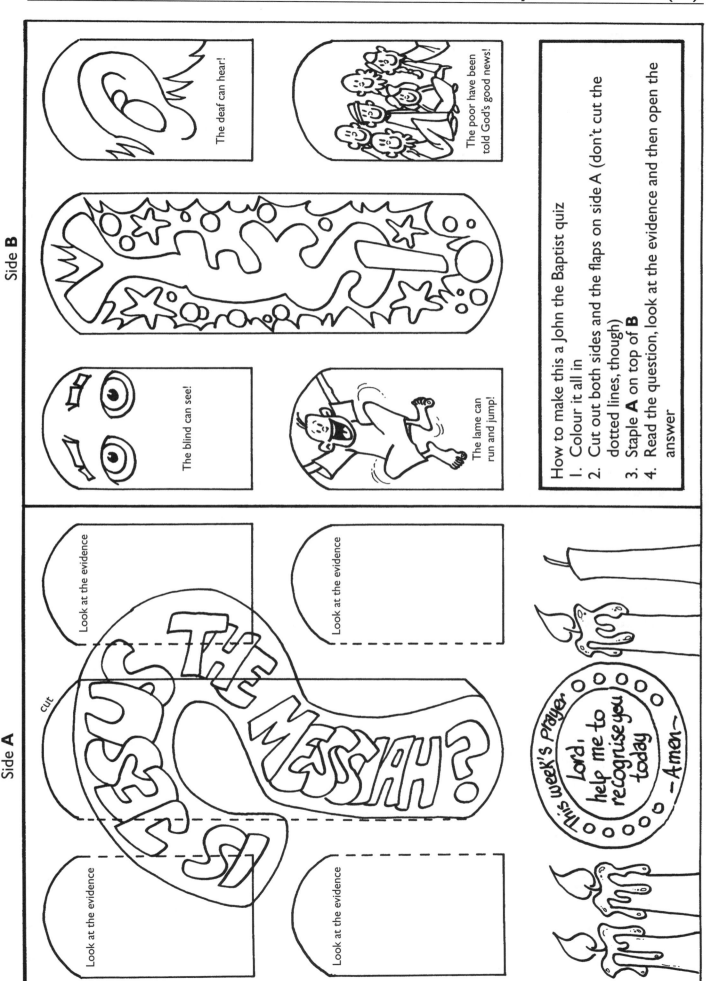

FOURTH SUNDAY OF ADVENT

Thought for the day

Through the willing participation of Mary and Joseph, God is poised to come among his people as their Saviour.

Readings

Isaiah 7:10-16
Psalm 80:1-7, 17-19
Romans 1:1-7
Matthew 1:18-25

Aim

To learn about the events leading up to Christmas from Joseph's point of view.

Starter

All change. Everyone sits in a circle and is given a number. The leader calls out any two numbers (or throws them on two dice) and these people have to change places. When the leader calls out, 'Calculator!' everyone changes places.

Teaching

In the game we all had to keep changing places. Today we are going to hear about the way Joseph had to cope with some big changes in his life.

Dress two of the children up as Joseph and Mary, and let the others work out who they are. At each 'scene' display a logo, based on the drawings below.

Scene 1: Mary's news

Have Mary and Joseph sitting together talking, and explain how one day Mary, who was going to marry Joseph, met him and told him she was going to have a child – an angel had come to tell her about it and now she was expecting the baby, which would be God's Son.

Scene 2: Help!

Joseph went off on his own and thought about it. He wasn't certain about Mary's story as it sounded so strange. But he decided to divorce her without a big fuss, to make it easier for her.

Scene 3: Sweet dreams

Joseph went home and got into bed. He lay and worried about Mary and the baby, and then he fell asleep. He had a dream in which he felt God was telling him it was fine to marry Mary and look after her and the baby.

Scene 4: Joseph woke up and remembered his dream

Suddenly he wasn't worried any more. Never mind if his friends thought him wrong and stupid – he knew that God really had used Mary to help him in his plan and now God wanted to use him as well. Joseph was needed to work with God in loving Mary and Jesus and looking after them both very carefully. Joseph told God he was happy to do it.

Scene 5: Joseph went to find Mary

He told her that he definitely believed her now, and would like to marry her straightaway!

Praying

Here I am, Lord,
ready to work with you
however you like.
Lead on and I'll follow! Amen.

Activities

On the worksheet there is an activity to help them 'reflect' on today's teaching, using a mirror. They can also create a collage for the children's area in church which shows Joseph and Mary on their way to Bethlehem. Use your own ideas or the outline suggested in the drawing below.

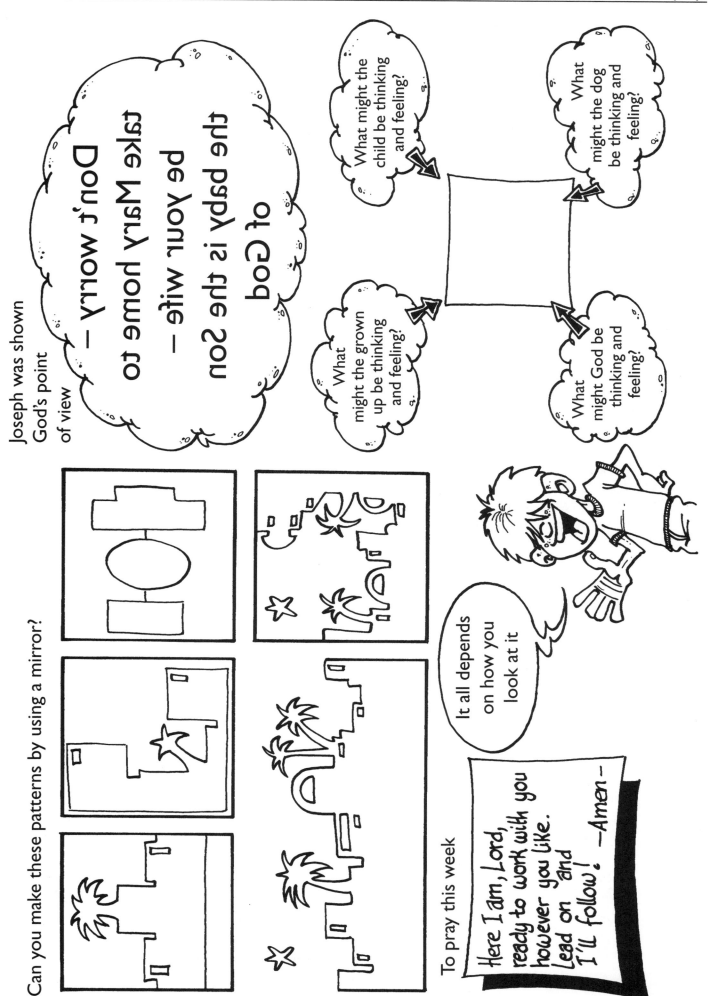

Joseph was shown God's point of view

Don't worry — take Mary home to be your wife — the baby is the Son of God

What might the child be thinking and feeling?

What might the dog be thinking and feeling?

What might the grown up be thinking and feeling?

What might God be thinking and feeling?

Can you make these patterns by using a mirror?

It all depends on how you look at it

To pray this week

Here I am, Lord, ready to work with you however you like. Lead on 'and I'll follow! —Amen—

CHRISTMAS

CHRISTMAS DAY

Thought for the day

The Word of God is made flesh. In the birth of Jesus we see God expressed in human terms.

Readings

Isaiah 52:7-10
Psalm 98
Hebrews 1:1-4 (5-12)
John 1:1-14

Activities

Christmas Day is very much a time for all God's children to worship together.

Involve all the children in the singing and playing of carols, decorating the church, and in the other ministries of welcoming, serving, collection of gifts and so on.

I have included a drawing and colouring activity for today so that children in church can work at this during the sermon.

Notes

FOLD

CUT OUT

CUT

FOLD

1. Colour the picture

2. Cut out the star and the outline

3. Colour the other side of this part brown, like the back of a stable

4. Fold at **a** and **b**

5. Stand up model in front of a light so the starlight shines in

AND THEY LAID HIM IN A MANGER

a

b

First Sunday of Christmas

Thought for the day

Jesus, the expression of God's love, lives as a vulnerable boy in the real and dangerous world we all inhabit.

Readings

Isaiah 63:7-9
Psalm 148
Hebrews 2:10-18
Matthew 2:13-23

Aim

To get to know the events of Matthew's account of Jesus' birth and the escape into Egypt.

Starter

Shh! Sit in a circle with one person blindfolded in the centre. Someone starts to walk around the circle carrying something noisy, such as a bunch of keys. The person in the centre tries to hear where they are. If they point to the right place, they get to carry the keys and someone else is blindfolded.

Teaching

Tell the escape story from today's Gospel with everyone making the sound effects and miming the actions. Everyone lies asleep, wakes up, yawns, listens, packs secretly, opens and closes the door very carefully, walks through the town without making any noise at all, looks around whenever there's a noise in case it's Herod, and shouts 'Yes!' when they eventually reach Egypt. Show them on a map where Bethlehem is in relation to Egypt, and then trace the return journey, reading from Matthew the reason given for not returning to Bethlehem.

Praying

Lord, keep us safe
as we travel through life.
Help us to love what is good
and hate what is evil. Amen.

Activities

On the sheet there are instructions for making a travelling game, which they can then play. They will need card and a dice for each game.

Notes

Colour the game

Stick it on card

TODDLER TRAVEL

Jesus did a lot of travelling when he was a toddler. In this game you can travel with him and Mary and Joseph, using counters and a dice. Joseph looked after his family and kept them safe. God looked after all of them!

To pray this week

Lord, keep us safe as we travel through life. Help us to love what is good and hate what is evil. —Amen—

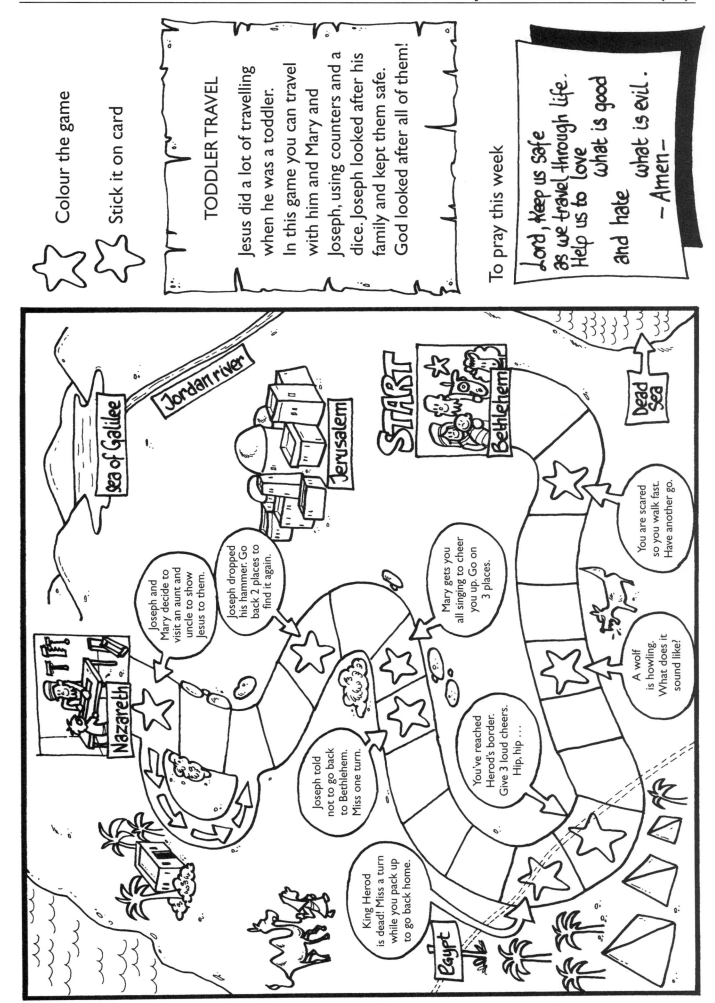

SECOND SUNDAY OF CHRISTMAS

Thought for the day

The grace and truth revealed in Jesus show God's freely-given love; through Jesus, God pours out his blessings on us and gives us real freedom.

Readings

Ecclesiasticus* 24:1-12 (* also called Sirach)
Canticle: Wisdom of Solomon 10:15-21
Ephesians 1:3-14
John 1:(1-9) 10-18

Aim

To know that Jesus is sometimes known as the Word of God.

Starter

Have a news session, with the children sitting in a circle and passing round a special stone (or Christmas decoration) so that the one holding it can speak while the others listen. This draws attention to the importance of listening to what is spoken, and helps to focus their attention.

Teaching

Point out that we have all been speaking out, or expressing our thoughts. Then tell them you are going to read them something and you want them to listen out for someone speaking, and what the result was of the word they spoke. Read Genesis 1:1-3. See if they can work out that it was through the word God spoke into the darkness that light first appeared and creation could begin to unfold.

Now read them the first three verses from John. Can they spot the same idea? Show a picture from a Christmas card of the Nativity. And ask them a really difficult question to get their brains going: Which person in this picture spoke out, or expressed God's love for us all? The one who did this completely was the baby in the manger – Jesus! So in a way, as St John says, Jesus is the Word of God. He is God speaking out his love to us all.

Make them feel very impressed with themselves because today they have been doing a spot of something called Theology, and they've done it very well!

Praying

Word of the Father,
now in flesh appearing.
O come, let us adore him,
Christ the Lord. Amen.

Activities

Using the guidelines on the sheet and a variety of felt-tips or coloured pencils, they will be writing out the first half of John 1:14 and decorating it to display. There is also a puzzle to help them look at what the word 'word' can mean.

Notes

Write in their words!

WORDS – WORDS – WORDS – WORDS – WORDS – WORDS
Unjumble the words to see all the things 'WORD' can mean

MESSAGE
PROMISE
EXPRESSION
NEWS
COMMAND
NAME

1. _____
2. _____
3. _____
4. _____
5. _____
6. _____

In medieval times the monks wrote out the words of the Bible by hand, and decorated their work.

The Word became flesh and lived among us.

JOHN 1:14

EPIPHANY

THE EPIPHANY

Thought for the day

Jesus, the hope of the nations, is shown to the world.

Readings

Isaiah 60:1-6
Psalm 72:(1-9) 10-15
Ephesians 3:1-12
Matthew 2:1-12

Aim

To explore why the wise men made their journey and what they found out.

Starter

Who am I? Fix a picture of an animal or food item on everyone's back. They have to find out who they are by going round asking questions about themselves. The others can only answer yes or no.

Teaching

Point out how in the game they had to search for the right answer, and it was like a journey to find the truth. Sometimes people were helpful in that and sometimes they weren't. Today we are looking at some wise men who set out on a quest.

Have two or three adults meeting up as if they are resting on the journey and chatting together about what the day has been like, what they miss, and what they are hoping to find. It is best to try out the conversation beforehand but without any set words as it will then sound natural.

When the wise men have settled down for the night (or gone to feed the camels), show the children a sheet of paper with these headings on it: Who? What? Why? In the different sections brainstorm ideas about who they were (wise men from the East), what they were doing (following a star to find a baby king of great importance) and why they bothered (they had worked out from the signs that this birth was really important for the human race, and they felt a strong urge to be there and pay their respects). Use the children's words, of course.

Now have the wise men on their way back, talking about how they felt about King Herod, what it was like to see Jesus, and why they are going home by a different route.

Praying

Have some incense, gold and myrrh on display during the teaching. As each is brought to the front pray together:

Gold
The wise men brought gold to Jesus.
Jesus, we bring you the gold of our obedience.
Help us to live as you want us to. Amen.

Frankincense
The wise men brought frankincense to Jesus.
Jesus, we bring you the incense of our worship.
You are God and we worship you. Amen.

Myrrh
The wise men brought myrrh to Jesus.
Jesus, we bring you the myrrh of the world's sadness.
Help us to look after one another better. Amen.

Activities

You will need lots of lining paper or rolls of wallpaper. The best present we can give to Jesus is ourselves. Working in twos, the children draw round each other on the paper, cut themselves out and colour them. On the front write:

Jesus,
the best present
I can give you
is myself!

The cut-outs can be offered with the gifts in church and given back at the end of the service for the children to remember at home.

The worksheet has a sequencing activity to consolidate the teaching, and a look at our own journey to Jesus.

Notes

over here

The wise men come to see Jesus

Colour these pictures, cut them out and stick them in the right order ...

Where are you on your journey to find Jesus? Have you found him yet? Draw in yourself where you feel you are.

R	S	K
E	F	I
N	C	A

SAM BOY TURNS RIGHT
Take every third letter

THE BAPTISM OF CHRIST: FIRST SUNDAY OF EPIPHANY

Thought for the day

As Jesus is baptised, the Spirit of God rests visibly on him, marking him out as the One who will save his people.

Readings

Isaiah 42:1-9
Psalm 29
Acts 10:34-43
Matthew 3:13-17

Aim

To get to know Matthew's account of Jesus' baptism.

Starter

Have a look at some atlases, picture books and travel brochures to find out where the River Jordan is and what it looks like.

Teaching

Wrap a 'camel hair shirt' round someone and stand him in the River Jordan (barefoot on a blue sheet). Can they guess who this is? If not, introduce them to John the Baptist, whom we met a couple of weeks before Christmas. Remind them that John is using the water as a sign of the people drowning to their old sinful lives and coming up with their sins forgiven by God, so they are clean and ready for when the Messiah comes. The Messiah, or Christ, is God's anointed one who will come and save his people.

Today we hear what happened when Jesus himself came to the River Jordan. He was about thirty years old at the time. (Have someone to be Jesus, walking into the river.) He asks John to baptise him, but John feels it ought to be the other way round. (Why?)

But Jesus persuades him that it is right for him to be baptised with everyone else, so John does it. (They act this out.) As soon as Jesus has been baptised, it's as if the heavens open up, and God's Spirit comes down to rest on him. It looks like a dove flying down to him. And there is a voice from heaven which says, 'This is my Son, whom I love; I am well pleased with him!' Have the words displayed so that everyone can say them together.

Praying

Jesus, I believe and trust
that you are God's Son,
the promised Saviour,
the Christ, the Messiah of God. Amen.

Activities

The worksheet helps them to make the connections between the prophecy in Isaiah and the words spoken at Jesus' Baptism, and there are instructions for making a dove out of salt dough. Here is the salt dough recipe: two cups of flour, one cup of salt, water to mix.

Notes

Isaiah the prophet wrote this many years before Jesus was alive.

'Here is my _____ whom I uphold, my _____ one in whom I _____ ;'

Isaiah 42:1

What's the link?

Find the words God speaks about Jesus

'This is my _____

Matthew 3:17

CHRIST = ANOINTED ONE
MESSIAH = ANOINTED ONE
GOD'S CHOSEN ONE

To pray this week

Jesus,
I believe and trust that you are God's Son, the promised Saviour, the Christ, the Messiah of God!
—Amen—

What you do:
1. Roll out dough ¼ cm thick
2. Cut round the template very carefully
3. Make a hanging hole and press patterns into the dove
4. Bake at a moderate temperature
5. When cool, paint with white paint mixed with PVC glue

How to make a dove to hang on the wall

You will need:

a lump of salt dough

a rolling pin

a template (see above)

white paint

PVC glue

SECOND SUNDAY OF EPIPHANY

Thought for the day

Jesus is recognised and pointed out by John to be God's chosen one.

Readings

Isaiah 49:1-7
Psalm 40:1-11
1 Corinthians 1:1-9
John 1:29-42

Aim

To get to know John's account of the disciples meeting Jesus and deciding to follow him.

Starter

Divide the children into pairs, giving each pair one half of an old Christmas card. One of the pair goes looking for the hidden piece of the picture and when they have seen it, they leave it where it is and go and sit down at one end of the room, saying nothing. Meanwhile the others are sitting at the other end of the room, following their partner with their eyes. At a given signal, once everyone is back, the group with one half of the picture go to the hidden part, collect it and join their partner. The first pair with the completed picture wins.

Teaching

Talk about how their partners had shown them exactly where to find what they wanted, so they were able to go straight to it, without wasting any time. Today we are going to find out how some people were helped by their friends to find someone they were looking for.

Using the carpet tiles method, let the children help to build up a picture of a road, some houses and trees (palm and sycamore), lake and distant hills. We are in Galilee about two thousand years ago. Go through the account in John's Gospel, with cut-out pictures of John the Baptist, Jesus, Andrew and his unnamed friend, Simon Peter, Philip and Nathanael. You can base these on the pictures below. (Beforehand practise talking through the events and moving the characters around with John's Gospel beside you as your 'script'.)

Talk with the children about the way we always want our friends to share any good news, and that's what happened here.

Praying

Jesus, I want my friend . . .
to meet you and find out how good it is
to live in your company. Amen.

Activities

On the sheet there is a friendship quiz, and instructions for making a friendship chain to help them pray for their friends.

Notes

ARE YOU A GOOD FRIEND?

1. Your friend needs you to help clear up after a party. Do you
   a) tell them you don't want to
   b) help them a bit but moan all the time
   c) have fun working at it together

2. You and your friend are with a group. They start being nasty to your friend. Do you
   a) join in
   b) keep quiet
   c) stick up for your friend

3. When you go round to play with your friend you like to watch a video and they like to play in the garden. Do you
   a) always make them watch the video
   b) find something else you both like to do
   c) sometimes play in the garden and sometimes watch a video

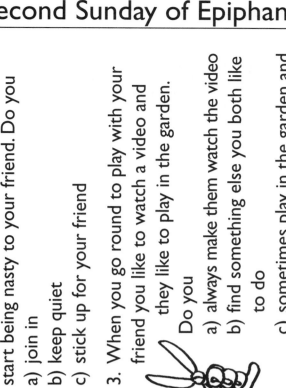

To pray this week

JESUS, I WANT MY FRIEND
TO MEET YOU AND FIND OUT
HOW GOOD IT IS
TO LIVE IN YOUR
COMPANY. —Amen—

How to make a friendship chain

1. Cut along the line

2. Fold the paper backwards and forwards

3. Cut round the person (leave the hands joined)

4. Open it up. It will look like this:

5. Colour them in to look like your friends

6. You can use your friendship chain to pray for them

CUT

THIRD SUNDAY OF EPIPHANY

Thought for the day

The prophecies of Isaiah are fulfilled in a new and lasting way in Jesus of Nazareth.

Readings

Isaiah 9:1-4
Psalm 27:1, 4-9
1 Corinthians 1:10-18
Matthew 4:12-23

Aim

To see that Isaiah's prophecy is fulfilled in Jesus.

Starter

Use this puzzle which contains two solutions at once:

CLUES

1. The capital city of Judea.
2. We listen with these.
3. A prophet from Jerusalem.
4. It will come, but hasn't yet.
5. What God can do for all captives.
6. Who fulfilled Isaiah's words? (The answer is already there, but we might not have understood it before.)

SOLUTION

```
        6.
1.    J E R U S A L E M
2.    E A R S
3.  I S A I A H
4.  F U T U R E
5.    S E T   F R E E
```

Teaching

Use a length of string as a time line to help the children understand the time scale. Have today's date hung at one end, Abraham at the other, Jesus in the middle. Then hang Isaiah's name about two-thirds of the way along from Abraham to Jesus.

Explain that a prophet is someone who speaks out God's Word. Sometimes, but not always, this will mean telling people about things which are going to happen. Isaiah was a prophet who spoke out God's Word in Jerusalem about 740 years before Jesus was born. He told the people of Israel about the fair and good way of living that God expected from his people, and looked forward to a time when God's light would shine out all over our world which is so often darkened with evil and unfairness. (Collect suggestions about some of the evil and unjust things that happen.)

Read the section of Isaiah's prophecy which is today's reading, and then find on a map the places mentioned. Now for a question: Who do they know about who did walk about Galilee bringing light into people's lives? Jesus did! Read the passage from Matthew and see if they can spot the bit from Isaiah.

Praying

Thank you, Lord, for using Isaiah
to help us recognise Jesus
as your Son.
Thank you for making it possible
for us all to be free. Amen.

Activities

On the worksheet there is a message which only looks right if you look at it from the right angle, to help them explore the idea of looking at things in different ways to get to the deeper meaning. There are also instructions for making a spinner which only makes the complete colour when it is spun round so that all the separate colours merge together.

Notes

How to make a spinner

Put all the colours together and make white!

You will need

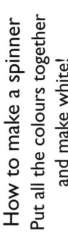

cotton

thin card

glue

red, blue and green coloured pencils

blutack

How to make it

1. Cut the circle out of the worksheet
2. Stick it on card
3. Colour both sides the right colours
4. Put the blutack behind the dots and push pencil through to make holes
5. Thread the cotton through one hole and out the other to make a long loop
6. Swing it round and round holding one end in each hand
7. Stop swinging it round and allow it to spin. Watch the colours merge together and make white

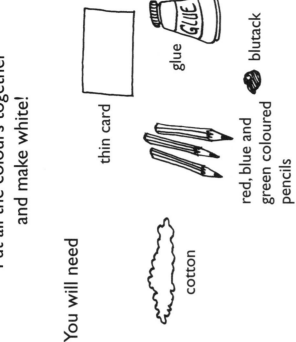

and remembered what the prophets said about the Messiah

They build put 2 together

When people looked at Jesus

red

green

blue

To pray this week

Thank you, Lord, for using Isaiah to help us recognise Jesus as your Son. Thank you for making it possible for us all to be free. – Amen –

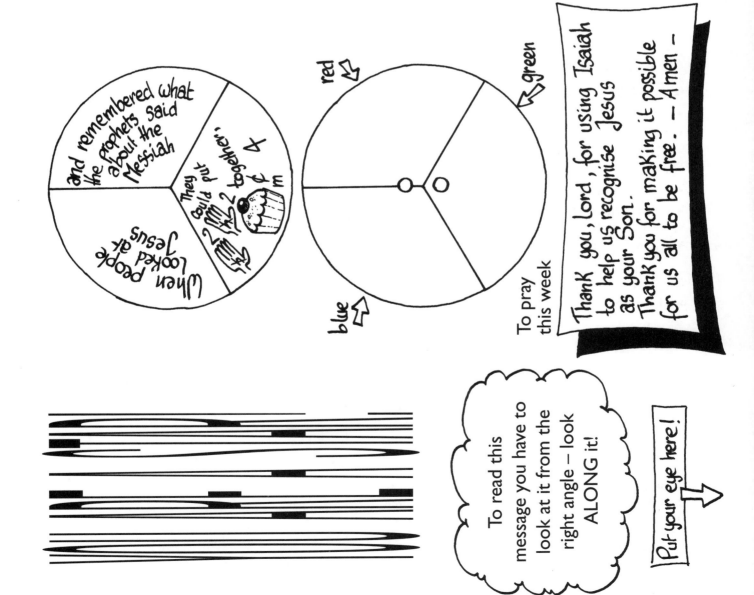

To read this message you have to look at it from the right angle – look ALONG it!

Put your eye here!

FOURTH SUNDAY OF EPIPHANY

Thought for the day

Jesus shows us in action the loving provision of the God who made us.

Readings

1 Kings 17:8-16
Psalm 36:5-10
1 Corinthians 1:18-31
John 2:1-11

Aim

To explore the meaning of the story in John's Gospel of the water that became wine.

Starter

Around the room have some pictures of raw materials and other pictures of things made from them. Here are some ideas:

- trees . . . furniture
- flour, eggs, margarine and eggs . . . a cake
- a sheep . . . a sweater
- wheat . . . a loaf of bread
- bees on flowers . . . a pot of honey
- a roll of fabric, thread, needle and scissors . . . a shirt or dress
- a lump of clay . . . a mug or jug

The children have to work out which goes with which. An alternative to having the pictures on the wall is to fix them to people's backs, so that they end up in matching pairs.

Teaching

We have been looking at where things come from. Today we are going to look at some water which turned into wine. (Show a jug of fresh water, and a carafe or bottle of wine.) This is a story about Jesus which is told to us in John's Gospel.

Use the script on page 132, and have two of the leaders, or primed visitors, dressed as servants (S1 and S2). (You could use a shepherd's costume from the Nativity costumes, or a dressing gown with a tea towel as the head-dress.) The servants are pretending to wash up after the wedding.

Praying

Lord God, there are so many wonderful things in your creation that we take for granted. Open our eyes to see it all as an expression of your love for us, and help us to live thankfully. Amen.

Activities

On the sheet there are instructions for making a stand-up 3D picture of the wedding at Cana. A puzzle helps the children explore some of the ideas which John is alerting us to by the story.

Notes

In the wedding story
John wants us to see ...

GOD'S POWER SEEN IN JESUS?

G OD GIVE SUSW HAT WEN EED

9, 1, 13, 14, 11, 4 / 6, 12 / 10, 9, 4 /

2, 6, 5 / 8, 6, 11, 1, 3, 7, 4

A	B	C	E	G	I	L	M	N	O	R	S	T	U
1	2	3	4	5	6	7	8	9	10	11	12	13	14

To pray this week

Lord God, there are so many
wonderful things in your creation
that we take for granted.
Open our eyes to see it all
as an expression of your love for us
and help us
to live thankfully.
—Amen—

How to make a
stand-up model

1. Colour all the pieces
2. Cut out carefully
3. Slot **a** in to **A**
4. Fold at the fold lines
5. Stand the title up
   beside it

'Do whatever
Jesus tells you'

cut A

fold

fold

a

ORDINARY TIME
PROPER 1

Sunday between 3 and 9 February inclusive
(if earlier than the Second Sunday before Lent)

Thought for the day

We are commissioned to live so that we shine like lights which direct others on to God, the source of Light.

Readings

Isaiah 58:1-9a (9b-12)
Psalm 112:1-9 (10)
1 Corinthians 2:1-12 (13-16)
Matthew 5:13-20

Aim

To look at how we can be salt and light in the world.

Starter

Together scatter tables and chairs around the room and then make the area as dark as possible. Everyone walks around, trying not to bump into any objects or people. Now switch on a light, or have a few torches available, so everyone can see where they are going.

Teaching

Talk about how useful light is, as it helps us see so that we don't bump into things. It helps us to see where we are going. Now read them the section from today's Gospel about light and salt, with parts of each displayed on sheets labelled 'Salt' and 'Light' as the words are read. Explain how light and salt are both things which allow good things to happen. Salt allows the full flavour of something to come out, and light allows people to see clearly so that they don't bump into things and hurt themselves.

So how can we be salt and light?

On the 'Salt' and 'Light' sheets, write down their suggestions. How can we behave so that people feel confident and happy in our company? How can we help to bring God's light into a frightening or wrong situation?

Praying

Help us, Lord,
to be salt in the world,
bringing out the best in people
by our love and respect for them.
And help us to be light in the world,
shining with your truth and goodness. Amen.

Activities

On the activity sheet there are suggestions for ways of being salt and light in different situations, and a puzzle which looks at the things God wants us to get involved with, which are spelt out in the Isaiah reading. There are instructions for making a doily so the 'salt' message is made clear. Have some crisps to put out on plates lined with the doilies. The children can hand these round after the service.

Notes

Some are both!

Draw a circle round the LIGHT ideas

Draw a square round the SALT ideas

forgiving someone who has made you late for your club

standing up for someone when they have been bullied

listening carefully when someone talks to you

remembering someone's birthday

asking someone if they would like some help

signing a petition to help a wrong to be put right

ISAIAH 58

with those who go hungry

to help your own relatives

to those who are cold and poor

those imprisoned by poverty

into your own homes

welcome the homeless

set free

give clothes

Don't refuse

share your food

BE LIKE SALT... BE LIKE SALT... BE LIKE SALT... BE LIKE SALT...

Help us, Lord, to be salt in the world, bringing out the best in people by our love and respect for them. And help us to be light in the world, shining with your truth and goodness. Amen.

Colour in and cut out. Place on plate.
Put crisps on top. Offer them round.

PROPER 2

Sunday between 10 and 16 February inclusive
(if earlier than the Second Sunday before Lent)

Thought for the day

To live God's way is to choose the way of life.

Readings

Deuteronomy 30:15-20 or Ecclesiasticus 15:15-20
Psalm 119:1-8
1 Corinthians 3:1-9
Matthew 5:21-37

Aim

To see that the ten commandments (God's way) are choosing life rather than death.

Starter

Scissors, stone, paper. In pairs everyone counts, 'One, two, three, GO!' and then chooses to show paper, stone or scissors to their partner. Paper is an open hand, stone a clenched fist and scissors two fingers opening and closing.

- Paper wins over stone (because it wraps it up).
- Stone wins over scissors (because it can smash them).
- Scissors wins over paper (because it can cut it).

Teaching

In that game we kept making choices, but we had no way of knowing whether they were going to be good choices or not. In the Old Testament God gave his people some rules to help them make good choices about the way to live.

Lay out ten objects to stand for the commandments, so they are easier to remember. Here are some suggestions, but choose whatever you think would work best for the children.

1. A figure 1, cut out of card. (Worship only the one true God and no other.)
2. An empty picture frame. (Don't make and worship pictures or models of God.)
3. A name tag. (Don't use God's name disrespectfully.)
4. A 'closed' shop sign. (Honour the Sabbath and keep it holy, resting from work on it.)
5. A photograph of a family. (Honour your father and your mother.)
6. A toy gun or sword. (Do not kill.)
7. A purse. (Do not steal.)
8. Wedding rings. (Don't steal other people's partners; be faithful in your relationships.)
9. Tape – video or sound. (Don't accuse people falsely or tell lies about them.)
10. Leaflets which advertise coveted items. (Don't keep wanting to have what other people have got.)

Go through the commandments in order, showing the objects and discussing the meaning as you go along. Then repeat them round the group, so everyone can use the visual clues to help them remember.

Praying

Whenever we turn away from you,
turn us back to face you,
so that we can live a lifetime
of love and truth. Amen.

Activities

Using the pattern on the activity sheet the children can make a 'chooser' with the suggested Bible references on it. There is also a scrambled roads puzzle to sort out so that they have to choose the best and safest route.

Notes

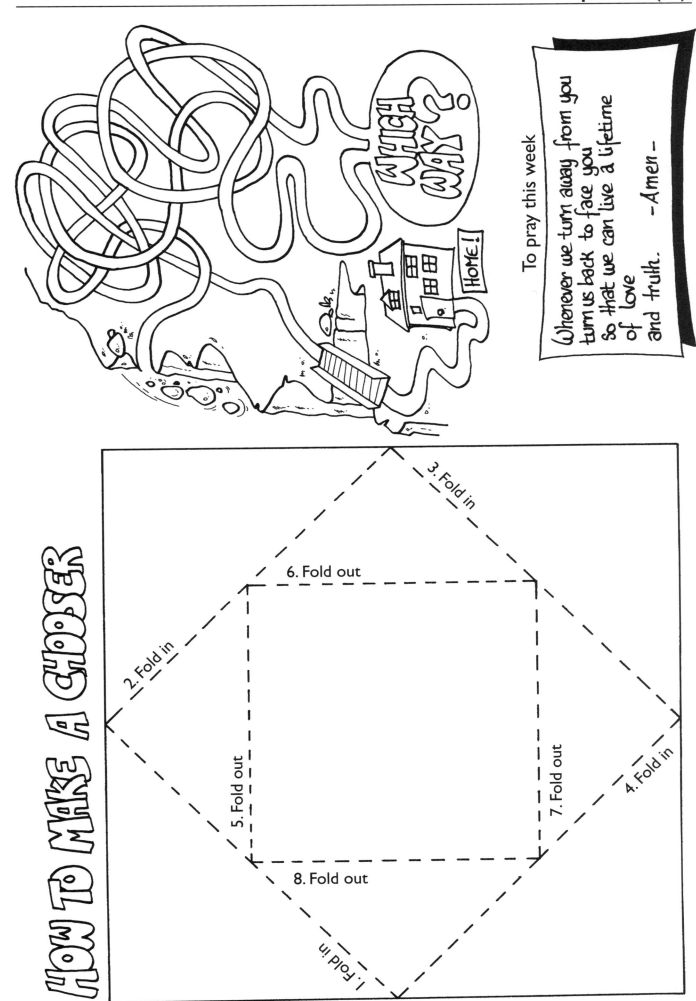

WHICH WAY?

Home!

To pray this week

Whenever we turn away from you
turn us back to face you
so that we can live a lifetime
of love
and truth.   —Amen—

HOW TO MAKE A CHOOSER

1. Fold in
2. Fold in
3. Fold in
4. Fold in
5. Fold out
6. Fold out
7. Fold out
8. Fold out

PROPER 3

Thought for the day

We are called to be holy; to be perfect in our generous loving, because that is what God our Father is like.

Readings

Leviticus 19:1-2, 9-18
Psalm 119:33-40
1 Corinthians 3:10-11, 16-23
Matthew 5:38-48

Aim

To know we are called to be loving and generous-hearted, like God.

Starter

Pass the ball. Stand in a circle with a ball – a large blow-up beach ball is good to use. If the children don't already know each other's names, go round saying these first. Then whoever has the ball says, 'Here you are, Laura', and throws the ball to her. Tell the children to make sure that everyone has the ball thrown specially to them, so that no one is left out.

Teaching

Talk about the fun of giving presents to people, both the wrapped-up sort we enjoy giving at Christmas and birthdays, and the little everyday presents like smiles and hugs, a crisp from our packet, a sweet from our bag, or our help with a job. Whenever we give in this loving way, we are being like God because he does it all the time. He loves giving us good things to enjoy and use. Using the carpet tiles as a background, add some pictures of the presents God gives, like sun and rain, fruiting trees, animals, people.

Now show a chart with ten faces on it, arranged in two groups of five. Explain how instead of loving one another, we tend to only love those we feel are 'on our side' by being in our family, our gang, or our country. And this is what happens: an eye for an eye, a tooth for a tooth. (Keep blacking out eyes and teeth in a tit-for-tat way, till all the faces end up blind and toothless.) Now let's listen to the teaching Jesus gave. Read Matthew 5:43-45, and across the picture of the faces write: 'Love your enemies'.

Praying

Jesus, this loving you talk about
is HUGE!
I know I don't always want to do it
but I can see it's a good idea.
Please help me to be better at it. Amen.

Activities

On the sheet there are instructions for making warm fuzzies to give away to people. The children will need wool for this. If you don't have any spare balls of wool, you can usually find some in charity shops quite cheaply. There are also instructions for making love stretch, using a pair of scissors and the chart provided.

Notes

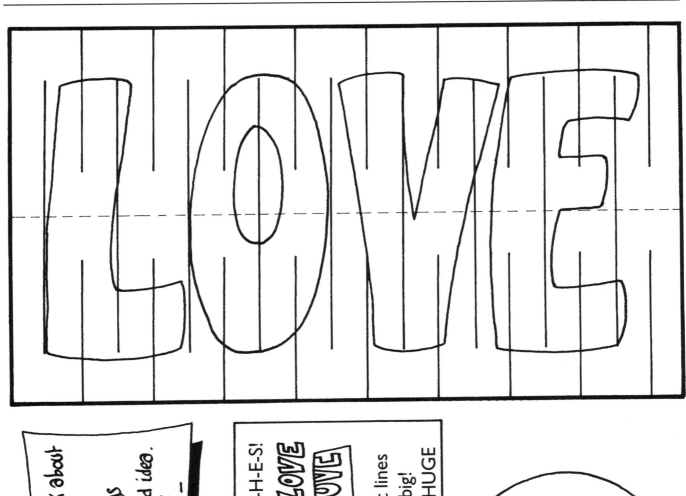

To pray this week

Jesus, this loving you talk about is HUGE! I know I don't always want to do it but I can see it's a good idea. Please help me to be better at it. —Amen—

LOVE S-T-R-E-T-C-H-E-S!

Colour the word *LOVE*

Fold the paper in half like this

Cut along all the cut lines

Open it out. Isn't it big!

GOD'S LOVE IS HUGE

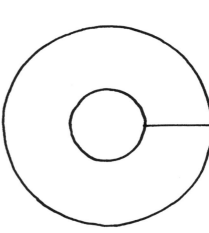

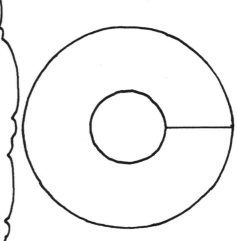

How to make a
Warm Fuzzy

1. Cut out the two circles below and put them together

2. Wind wool round and round like this

3. When it looks like this cut all round the edge

4. Tie some wool round the middle between the two paper circles

5. Pull off the paper and fluff out the warm fuzzy

6. Give it to someone you love!

SECOND SUNDAY BEFORE LENT

Thought for the day

God is creative and good; seeking his rule, as our priority, will mean that everything else falls into place.

Readings

Genesis 1:1-2:3
Psalm 136 or 136:1-9, 23-26
Romans 8:18-25
Matthew 6:25-34

Aim

To see God's love in his creation.

Starter

Use modelling clay to make something they are glad God has made. These can all be gathered on to a tray covered in green and blue paper.

Teaching

Prepare cut-outs of each creation day's work, which can be stuck on to a blank sheet of paper in order while the Genesis passage is being read. Use these ideas or design your own.

1. A plain sheet of black paper.

2. Sky blue paper to cover half of the top of the black paper. (You'll need to keep some of the 'sky' black.)

3. Shiny blue paper across the bottom part.

4. Brown land shape in the blue sea. Trees with fruit, flowers and grass.

5. Sun in the blue half of sky, moon and stars in the black side.

6. Birds and fish.

7. Animals and humans.

8. The title: 'God saw that it was very good.'

Have some music playing as a background, someone to read the creation story, and someone else to get on with the developing picture, so the narrative is not interrupted but interpreted as it goes along, and the children experience with several senses at once.

Our creative, loving God has given us all this. Isn't it beautiful! If God takes all this care over everything he makes, then we can be sure he will take great care of us, too. We don't need to waste our time worrying and being anxious, because our God is the powerful creative God who brought our whole universe into being and our planet into life.

Praying

Throw a ball which is designed to look like the earth, as you sing:

You've got the whole world in your hand,
you've got the whole wide world in your hand,
you've got the whole world in your hand,
you've got the whole world in your hand.

Activities

Have smaller versions of the large collage so the children can each make their own creation picture following the order given on the sheet. Arrange each set of items, ready cut, in different boxes so the children can work their way along, picking up one item from each box.

Notes

MAKE A CREATION PICTURE

Stick everything on in the right order. Then for '7' sit back and enjoy your picture!

1. Light and dark
2. Sky and sea
3. Land and plants
4. Sun, moon and stars
5. Birds and fish
6. Animals and humans

need!

Just

worry!

Don't

knows

heavenly

trust

Father

You've got the whole world in your hand,
You've got the whole wide world in your hand,
You've got the whole world in your hand,
You've got the whole world in your hand.

you

Your

him.

what

SUNDAY BEFORE LENT

Thought for the day

In Jesus the full glory of God is revealed and encountered.

Readings

Exodus 24:12-18
Psalm 2 or Psalm 99
2 Peter 1:16-21
Matthew 17:1-9

Aim

To get to know the story of the Transfiguration.

Starter

Eye-witnesses. As the children gather and are talking with the leaders exchanging news, have some events taking place, but without drawing attention to them. For instance, someone might carry two chairs across the room from one side to the other and back again. Someone might wheel a bike through, or walk across with glove puppets or a distinctive hat on. Gather everyone in a circle and see what people have noticed, including the colours and number of objects carried.

Teaching

Explain that we have a special guest today, who was an eye-witness to something that happened about two thousand years ago. Introduce Simon Peter (who could be an import for the occasion, or one of the helpers). If you want to dress him up, use one of the Nativity play costumes, or a stripy dressing-gown with tea-towel headdress.

You could use the script in the Appendix on page 133, but it's best if the main ideas are taken on board and the actual words left natural.

Praying

Glory to the Father and to the Son
and to the Holy Spirit,
as it was in the beginning, is now
and shall be for ever. Amen.

Activities

On the activity sheet there are instructions for making a stand-up model of the Transfiguration and a 'holy mountains' quiz for which the children will need access to a Bible.

Notes

slot 1
slot 2
cut out
cut out
Fold

cut slot
cut slot
slot 1
slot 2

ⓑ
ⓐ
Fold

Colour all the bits.
Cut and fold.
Stick **a** to **a** and **b** to **b**.
Fix the figures in the slots.

ⓑ

ⓐ

Jesus led them up a high mountain

Matthew 17:1-9

Genesis 8:3-4

Exodus 24:12-18

Mount Ararat, where Noah's ark settled as the flood went down

Mount Sinai, where God met with Moses and gave him the 10 commandments

The high mountain in Galilee where Jesus was transfigured as he prayed

To pray this week

Glory to the Father
and to the Son
and to the Holy Spirit,
as it was in the beginning,
is now
and shall be forever.
— Amen —

LENT

First Sunday of Lent

Thought for the day

Jesus knows all about temptation; and he can deal with our sin.

Readings

Genesis 2:15-17; 3:1-7
Psalm 32
Romans 5:12-19
Matthew 4:1-11

Aim

To know about Jesus' temptations in the desert.

Starter

Prepare some coloured pieces of paper and some white pieces with questions on. Stick them on to people with sticky tape. The questions have to team up with the right answers. Here are some suggestions:

What colour is a banana?	Blue
What colour is grass?	Yellow
What colour is the sky?	Black
What colour is coal?	Green

Teaching

Borrow some library books to show the children some pictures of the desert where Jesus went to be on his own with God after he had been baptised. Use a yellow or brown and a blue towel laid on the floor as the background to the story, and sit the children round the edge. Explain that to fast means to go without food, and people sometimes do this when they are praying, especially if they are wanting to find out God's will for them in their life.

After he had been baptised, Jesus went off into the desert to fast and pray. He wanted to make sure he was really listening to God as he didn't want to get it wrong. As you tell the story of the three temptations, place the following objects on the background:

1. A loaf of bread (stone shaped) and a large stone. (Satan was homing in on Jesus' feeling hungry: personal comfort and survival.)

2. A high tower built of bricks and a cut-out question mark. (Satan was picking up on Jesus wondering who he was and what his job would be exactly.)

3. A wrapped present and a bill or invoice. (Satan suggested a way for Jesus to give his Father a present – but it came with a crazy price tag.)

As you tell the story, place beside each set of objects the answers Jesus used:

1. Matthew 4, verse 4
2. Matthew 4, verse 7
3. Matthew 4, verse 10

Praying

Lord Jesus,
when I am tempted to do what is wrong
and unloving and selfish,
make me brave
and keep me strong. Amen.

Activities

On the activity sheet there are instructions for making a temptation wheel. Each child will need a split pin for this. The teaching is also reinforced by a puzzle to match up and look up the temptations and answers, and the children will need access to a Bible for this.

Notes

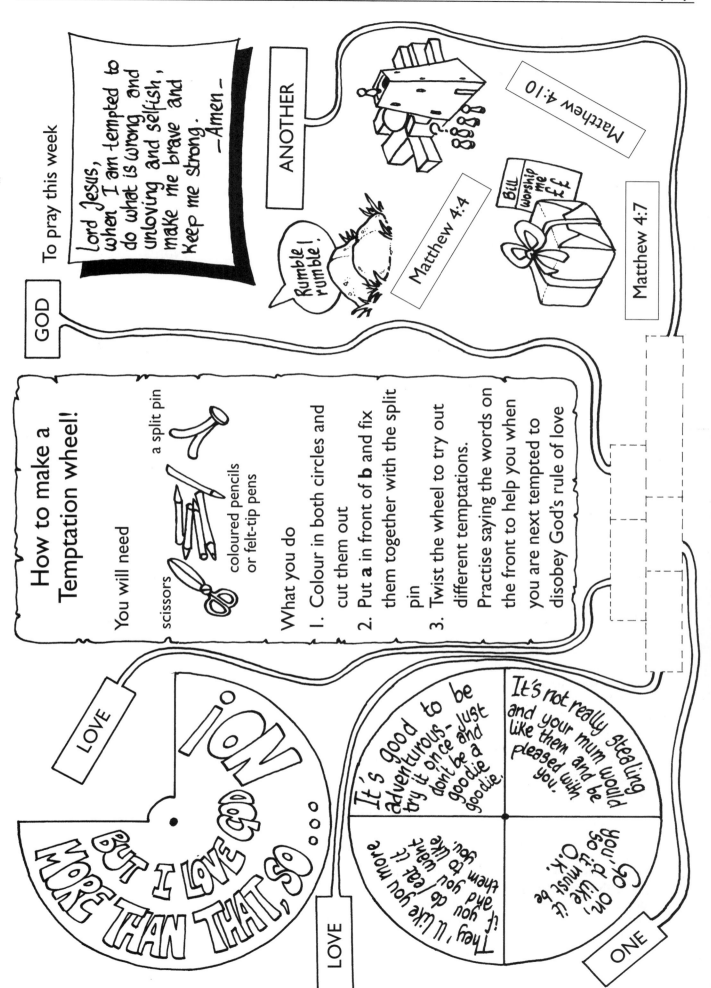

SECOND SUNDAY OF LENT

Thought for the day

Anyone who believes in Jesus can know his power to save and set us free.

Readings

Genesis 12:1-4a
Psalm 121
Romans 4:1-5, 13-17
John 3:1-17

Aim

To know that when Abram was called, he trusted God and went.

Starter

Follow my leader. Put on a children's praise tape and have different children leading the line with everyone following the leader in both method and direction.

Teaching

Talk about moving house and have everyone miming the furniture removal, packing and unpacking. Share in the group anyone's memories about how they felt when they moved and saw their home being emptied, and the new one filling up. Help them to sense that moving is quite an upheaval, often with some sadness at what we are leaving behind, but excitement at what we are moving on to. Pick up on the fear and adventure of going forward into the unknown.

Now drape a large cloth over some upturned basins to make a hilly landscape, and tell them about Abram, whose name God later changed to Abraham (marked on the landscape with a cardboard question mark), living happily settled when God called him to uproot and move on into the unknown. Describe the gathering, packing and moving, with the children making the noises of all the sheep, goats, cows, children (la, la, la) and grown-ups (natter, natter, natter) as the cross is moved over the landscape – rather like the wartime charts of progress. All the time Abram kept listening to God and checking where they should all be going. He trusted God completely. When we live closely in touch with God, and go along with his ideas, even if they take us into the unknown, we are living by faith – faith in a loving God who can be trusted.

Praying

Lord God, here is my life!
Lead me your way
and I will follow you
wherever and however you want. Amen.

Activities

There is a picture on the sheet for the children to complete of Abram and his family setting off, and a moving model to make through a landscape.

Notes

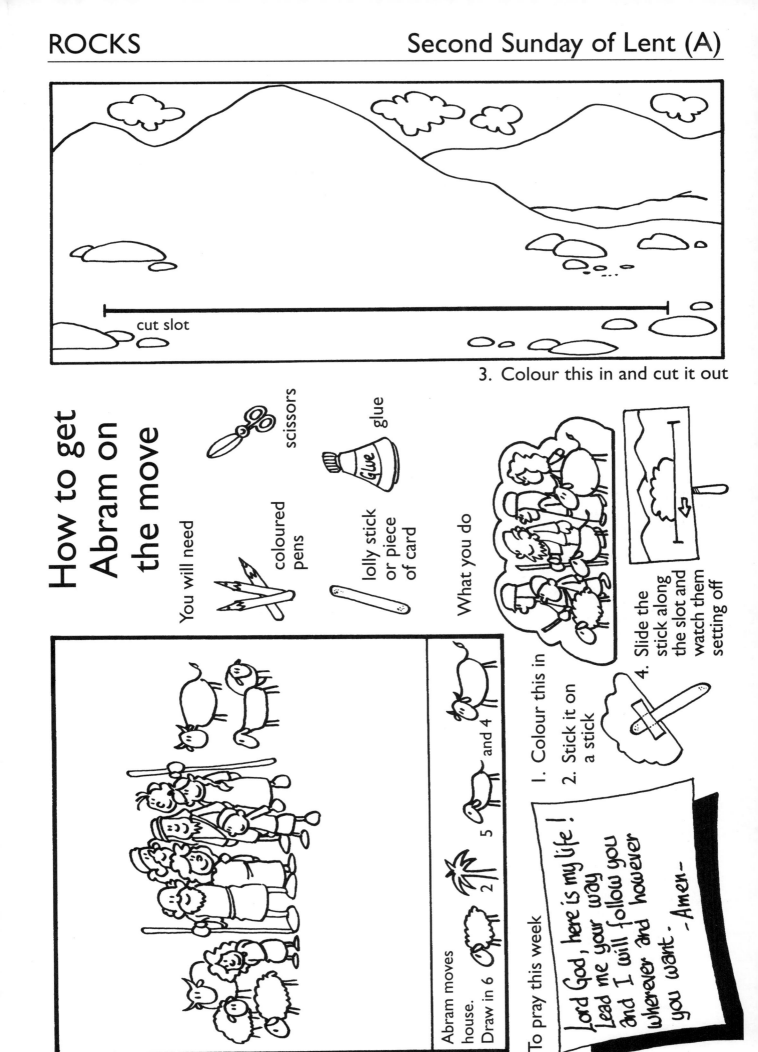

cut slot

3. Colour this in and cut it out

How to get Abram on the move

You will need

scissors

glue

coloured pens

lolly stick or piece of card

What you do

1. Colour this in

2. Stick it on a stick

4. Slide the stick along the slot and watch them setting off

Abram moves house.
Draw in 6 🐑 2 🌴 5 🐐 and 4 🐄

To pray this week

Lord God, here is my life !
Lead me your way
and I will follow you
wherever and however
you want. -Amen-

THIRD SUNDAY OF LENT

Thought for the day

God both knows us completely and loves us completely; meeting us where we are, he provides us with living water, to satisfy all our needs.

Readings

Exodus 17:1-7
Psalm 95
Romans 5:1-11
John 4:5-42

Aim

To know that Jesus is 'living water'.

Starter

Water from the well. Each team has a bucket of water at one end of the room and an empty washing-up bowl at the other. The teams have to get water from one end of the room to the other, without moving the containers. Each team member is given a small tub and can organise themselves however they wish. (Some may make a human chain, others may run from one end to the other.) If the weather is reasonable, this could be an outside activity.

A quieter, drier alternative starter is to have a water-tasting session, with some bottles of different types of water, their labels hidden, and some cups. The children can tick their favourites.

Teaching

Talk about the freshness of flowing or living water, and show a picture of some women of today collecting water for the family at the local fresh water well. Today we are going to listen in on a conversation which takes place nearly two thousand years ago, by a well in Samaria.

Use two or three women leaders or helpers, dressed in nativity costumes and carrying jars or jugs, to chat the conversation that one of them has had with Jesus. To prepare for this, read the passage through several times and make a note of the main direction of the conversation. Then the woman can tell the story to her friends with them pumping her with questions, and eventually going off to see Jesus for themselves. It is best done informally and unscripted as it then sounds natural, and if someone forgets something one of the others can remind them with a question. Link the need for water to Jesus calling himself 'living water', with the women working out what he meant by this.

Praying

Flow in me, living water of God,
and satisfy my needs.
Flow through me, living water of God,
to bring life and hope to the world.

Activities

On the sheet there are instructions for making a working model of a well. Each child will need a small plastic pot, a drinking straw with a wiggly end, some thin string and some card. There are also discussion starter pictures, showing areas in our world in need of God's living water.

Notes

Fourth Sunday of Lent: Mothering Sunday

Thought for the day

Thanking God for our earthly opportunities for mothering and being mothered, we also remember the mothering parenthood of God.

Readings

Exodus 2:1-10 or 1 Samuel 1:20-28
Psalm 34:11-20 or Psalm 127:1-4
2 Corinthians 1:3-7 or Colossians 3:12-17
Luke 2:33-35 or John 19:25-27

Activities

Today is not one for learning separately but for celebrating and learning together. Use some of the all-age suggestions from the *Living Stones* Complete Resource Book, involve the children and young people in the music group or choir, as servers, welcomers, collectors for the offering, and so on. Provide shakers and bells for the younger ones to play during one or two hymns, and streamers to wave. Gather the children round the altar for the eucharistic prayer and choose hymns where the language is accessible.

Notes

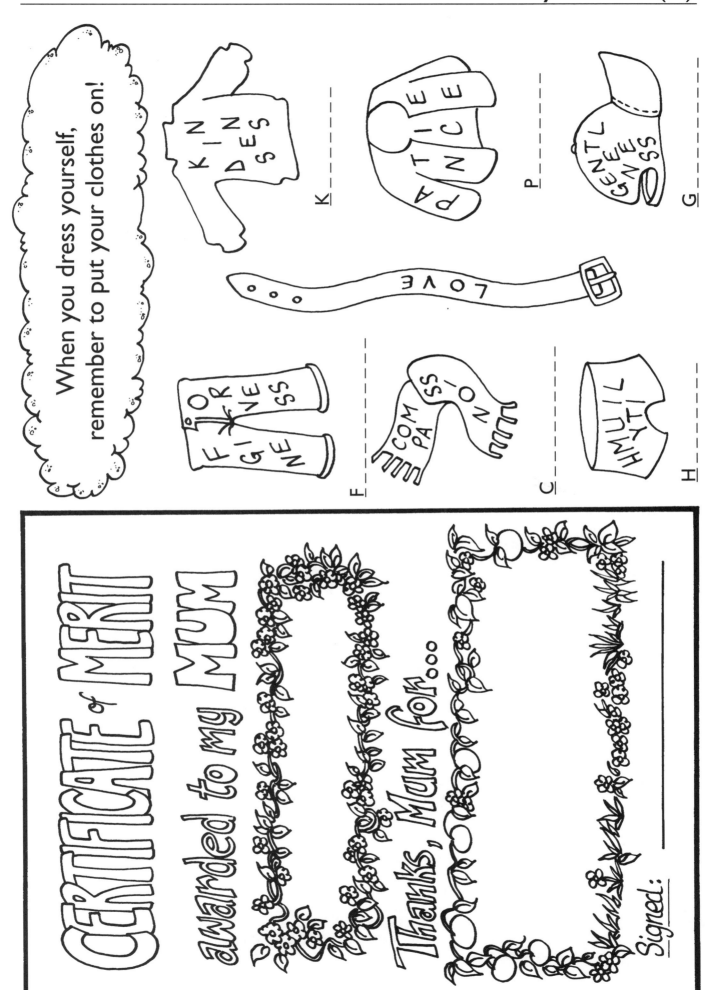

When you dress yourself, remember to put your clothes on!

KINDNESS K

PATIENCE P

GENTLENESS G

LOVE

FORGIVENESS F

COMPASSION C

HUMILITY H

CERTIFICATE of MERIT

awarded to my MUM

Thanks, Mum for...

Signed: _____

Fifth Sunday of Lent

Thought for the day

Jesus is the resurrection and the life. He can transform death and despair, in any form, into life and hope.

Readings

Ezekiel 37:1-14; Psalm 130
Romans 8:6-11; John 11:1-45

Aim

To know that Jesus is the resurrection and the life.

Starter

Play musical statues. Choose some appropriate music to play during the dancing, such as *Dem bones* (see Appendix, page 130, for the words and music), *Every minute of every day* or *The race*.

Teaching

Beforehand draw a large picture of a person and cut it up into pieces to match the number of people in the group. Give each person a piece of the puzzle and invite them a few at a time to add their section to complete the picture. As this happens read the children Ezekiel 37:1-6. When the picture is finished tell the children how God is able to put together again people who feel broken up by sadness or bad things that have happened to them. Even when everything seems hopeless, God can breathe in hope. There is nothing he can't use somehow, even the worst things.

Now get everyone involved in telling the story of Lazarus, most as the crowd of friends who are sad when he dies and amazed and happy when Jesus brings him back to life again. Either narrate the story in your own words, or use this script:

Jesus had some friends called Lazarus, Martha and Mary. He often stopped off at their house for a meal, and sometimes he'd stay with them. One day Lazarus got very ill. His sisters looked after him and gave him cool drinks, and mopped his hot head, and did everything they could to make him better, but Lazarus got worse and worse. Martha and Mary wished their friend Jesus was around to help, but Jesus was away in Jerusalem. Then a very sad thing happened. Lazarus got so ill that he died. Mary and Martha cried, and all their friends and neighbours were sad as well and tried to comfort them. 'At least he isn't in pain any more,' they said. That was true of course, but Mary and Martha just knew they loved their brother and wanted to have him back living with them again and for everything to be normal and ordinary.

Four days later Jesus returned with his disciples and Martha went out to meet him as soon as she heard he was on his way. When she saw him she burst out, 'If you had been here, Jesus, my brother wouldn't have died!' Then she stopped and thought a moment. Perhaps there was still hope even though Lazarus was dead. 'In fact,' she went on, 'I'm sure that even now God will give you anything you ask.' Jesus looked at Martha and saw her sadness, her love for her brother, and he saw that she really wanted to believe that Jesus was the Christ, the Son of God.

Then Martha ran back to the house and told Mary that Jesus was there. Mary went out, still crying, and met Jesus. She couldn't understand why this had happened when Jesus wasn't there to help and she said so to Jesus. Jesus looked at her and saw the ache of sadness in her heart. He saw her not understanding how a good God could let such terrible things happen. And Jesus sobbed and sobbed at the sadness of it all. They cried together. At last Jesus said, 'Where did you bury him?' Martha and all their friends had joined them now and they all said, 'Come and see.' They all walked until they came to the tomb where Lazarus had been laid. Some of the crowd realised how much Jesus loved his friend Lazarus. Other people couldn't understand why Jesus hadn't stopped his friend from dying.

Jesus gave the order for the stone that sealed up the tomb to be rolled away. Jesus looked up to heaven and prayed to his Father, thanking him for hearing his prayer and longing for the people to believe and understand. Then he called out loudly, 'Lazarus, come out!'

Everyone watched the tomb and heard the power of life in Jesus' voice. It was reaching right into death. And then there was a shuffling noise, and there was Lazarus, still wrapped up in his death clothes, but pulling them off and smiling as he walked out of the tomb, completely better and completely alive! Everyone gasped and took a step back in amazement, and then crowded round Lazarus, hugging him, some of them crying again – but this time for joy! That day many more people came to believe that Jesus was the Messiah they had been waiting for. He really was the Lord of life.

Praying

Lord Jesus, bring us all to life
by the power of your love.
Bring us all to live
in the life of your kingdom. Amen.

Activities

On the sheet there are instructions for making a jigsaw puzzle which reinforces today's teaching, and a wordsearch that includes the keywords and characters from the Lazarus story.

A	E	H	A	M	A	Z	E	D	G	C	Y
M	B	J	B	N	L	V	K	X	S	A	D
L	A	Z	A	R	U	S	F	C	T	I	W
U	A	P	V	A	C	O	H	J	O	E	U
Y	I	L	D	L	D	J	Z	E	H	M	X
M	T	D	I	E	D	E	V	R	G	T	E
M	C	C	S	V	R	S	F	U	S	O	G
A	O	R	E	N	E	U	Q	S	J	M	C
R	B	P	Y	K	Q	S	K	A	P	B	J
T	L	T	A	I	Z	D	N	L	O	U	T
H	A	P	P	Y	N	Q	F	E	I	R	V
A	U	M	X	R	S	G	W	M	A	R	Y

MARY   CRYING   DIED   JESUS   TOMB

MARTHA   LAZARUS, COME OUT   JERUSALEM

SAD

AMAZED   ALIVE   HAPPY   To pray this week

Lord Jesus, bring us all to life
by the power of your love.
Bring us all to live in the
life of your kingdom.
                              —Amen—

A jigsaw to make

1. Colour the picture carefully
2. Stick it on to thin card
3. Cut it up into pieces
4. As you put the pieces of your JIGSAW together,
   try putting the meaning together as well

PALM SUNDAY

Thought for the day

Jesus rides into Jerusalem cheered by the crowds. Days later crowds will be clamouring for his death.

Readings

Liturgy of the Palms:
Matthew 21:1-11
Psalm 118:1-2, 19-29

Liturgy of the Passion:
Isaiah 50:4-9a
Psalm 31:9-16
Philippians 2:5-11
Matthew 26:14-27:66 or Matthew 27:11-54

Aim

To look at why Jesus came riding into Jerusalem on a donkey.

Starter

If your church has a Palm Sunday procession the children will be joining in with this. Provide them with branches and flags to wave. Otherwise, have a procession with all the children and young people, making it lively and joyful with taped music, singing, dancing and percussion instruments.

Teaching

With the children's help go over the events of Jesus' life from his birth in Bethlehem and childhood in Nazareth in a country which was ruled over by the Romans. Mention Jesus' Baptism and his time of testing out in the wild country on his own. Mention his job as a carpenter and his ministry, bringing out that he healed those who were ill, or unable to walk or hear or speak or see, as well as telling the people about the way God loved them. He talked about the kingdom of God, or the kingdom of heaven. This wasn't so much a place as a way of living – the loving way of living. As the events are mentioned, draw or write them along a time line.

The people wanted to make Jesus their king, but the kind of king they had in mind would lead them to fight the Romans and throw them out of their country. Was this the kind of king Jesus was?

Tell the story of the entry into Jerusalem, first practising these sound effects, which can be used during the story:

- Donkey – 'hee-haw!' and tongue clicking for a 'clip, clop' noise

- Jesus – 'Hosanna to the son of David!'

- Jerusalem – 'Holy city of peace' (whispered)
- Palms – rub palms of hands together to sound like the wind in the trees
- Crowd – 'Jesus! Jesus! Jesus!' in a chant

Praying

You laid aside your majesty,
gave up everything for me,
suffered at the hands of those you had created.
You took all my guilt and shame
when you died and rose again,
now today you reign
in heaven and earth exalted.

(From a song by Noel Richards
© Copyright 1985 Kingsway's Thankyou Music.)

Activities

Following the instructions on the sheet, the children can make palm crosses. The other activities encourage them to see both the rejoicing as Jesus comes into Jerusalem and also the seriousness and sadness of Palm Sunday as he rides towards the cross.

Notes

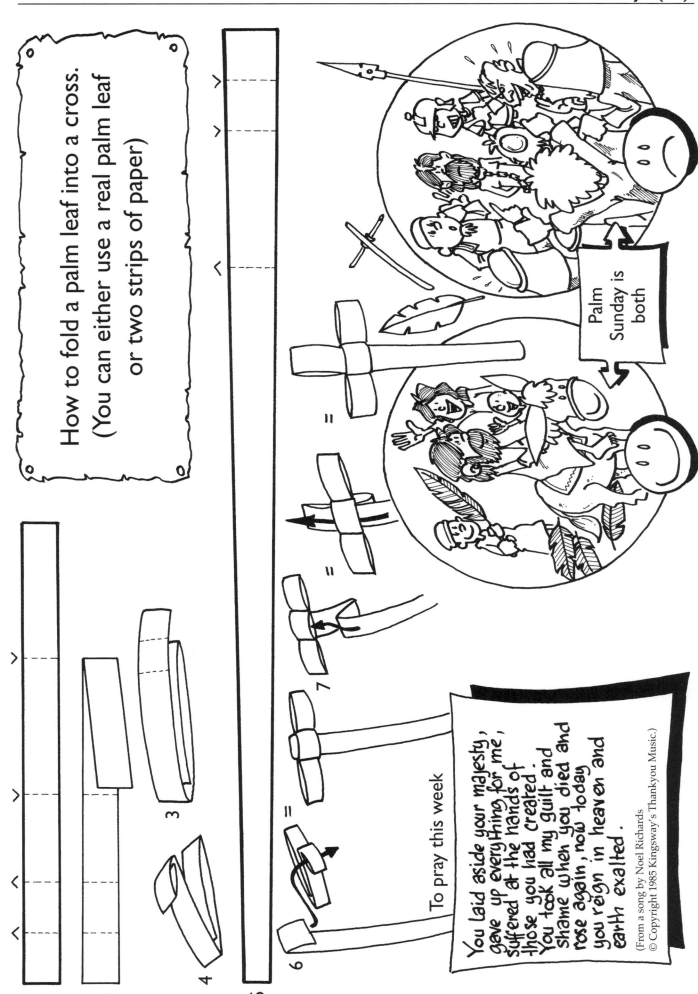

How to fold a palm leaf into a cross.
(You can either use a real palm leaf or two strips of paper)

Palm Sunday is both

To pray this week

You laid aside your majesty,
gave up everything for me,
suffered at the hands of
those you had created.
You took all my guilt and
shame when you died and
rose again; now today
you reign in heaven and
earth exalted.

(From a song by Noel Richards
© Copyright 1985 Kingsway's Thankyou Music.)

EASTER

EASTER DAY

If possible, it is recommended that the children and young people are in church with the other age groups today. Use and adapt some of the all-age ideas from the *Living Stones* Complete Resource Book, and involve the children in some of the music and in the cleaning and decorating of the church.

Thought for the day

It is true. Jesus is alive for all time. The Lord of life cannot be held by death. God's victory over sin and death means that new life for us is a reality.

Readings

Acts 10:34-43 or Jeremiah 31:1-6
Psalm 118:1-2, 14-24
Colossians 3:1-4 or Acts 10:34-43
John 20:1-18 or Matthew 28:1-10

Aim

To teach them about the first Easter.

Starter

Have an Easter egg hunt, preferably outside if this is safe and practical.

Teaching

Invite a man from the congregation into Living Stones this week to be Peter, and interview him about who he is, and what had happened on Friday. Then ask him what happened on the next Sunday morning. Here are some questions to give you an idea:

- Good morning! What's your name?
- Now you're a friend of this Jesus, aren't you?
- I've heard that last Friday he was put to death by the Romans. Is that right?
- I expect you were there with him through it all, being such a good friend?
- Well, what happened on Sunday morning? We've heard a lot of confusing reports!
- Is it possible that someone could have stolen Jesus' body?
- Now hang on a minute. You're saying that Jesus is alive again for ever. That must mean that he'll still be just as alive in about two thousand years' time! Is that right?
- Well, thank you, Peter, for coming this morning to tell us this amazing news. We'll be looking out for Jesus. It's really good to know he's still alive!

Praying

Christ has died. *(arms out)*
Christ has risen. *(arms up)*
Christ will come again! *(kneel on one knee, arms down, palms up)*

Activities

Give the children a large letter (at least A4 size) to colour and decorate. When they get back into church these letters can be held up or fixed up on the wall or laid on the floor to make the message: JESUS IS ALIVE FOR EVER!

Notes

How long will Jesus live for?

for ever and ever!

a few years

until the year 2000

YES

NO

NO

NO

QUESTION	NO	YES
Was Jesus born?		
Did he show God's love?		
Was he killed with stones?		
Did he die on a Roman cross?		
Did he stay dead?		

To pray this week

Christ has died
(arms out)
Christ has risen
(arms up)
Christ will come again!
(Kneel on one knee,
arms down, palms up)

JESUS IS ALIVE!

Second Sunday of Easter

Thought for the day

Through the risen Jesus we have a living hope which will never spoil or fade.

Readings

Acts 2:14a, 22-32; Psalm 16
1 Peter 1:3-9; John 20:19-31

Aim

To know what it was that convinced Thomas and the others that Jesus was alive.

Starter

Place a few objects in a 'feelie bag'. Show the bag and point out that at the moment we can't tell what is in it. Now pass it around the circle. Each person has a feel and tries to identify the contents, but must not say anything. When everyone has had a go, each person in turn has a chance to name one thing they think is in the bag. Empty the contents so that everyone can see whether they were right.

Teaching

Explain that in the last activity you could have told people what was in the bag, and they might have believed you and they might not. Would they have believed you if you had said there was a toothbrush in the bag? What about an elephant? Why are we more likely to believe some things than others? We use our common sense and our experience. If we have seen an elephant, we know that it wouldn't fit inside this bag, but a toothbrush would. Today we are going to hear about someone who found it very hard to believe that Jesus really was alive. In fact he said this: 'Unless I see the nail marks in his hands and put my finger where the nails were, and put my hand into his side, I will not believe it.' (Have this written up in a large speech bubble, so that all the children who can read can join in with the words.) The person's name was Thomas, and he was one of Jesus' disciples and loyal friends.

Now here is our first question: 'How likely do you think Thomas thought it was for him to be able to see and touch Jesus' wounds?' (Have a temperature chart headed, 'Thomas thought it was . . .' with these markings on it: impossible, very unlikely indeed, most unlikely, unlikely, possible, likely, very likely, dead certain.

Different children can come and point to the level they think. (There isn't a right or wrong answer, but it gets them thinking!)

Next: 'Thomas wished it could be true, because

he loved Jesus and missed him.' (Place this heading over the first with blutack.) Again, let various children come and point to the level they think.

Sometimes we believe things because we want them to be true. Who believes that (West Ham) will win their next game? Thomas didn't want to pretend to believe. He didn't want to kid himself. If it was really true that his friend Jesus was alive, then he would believe it and be very happy. If it wasn't, he'd rather face up to that. Perhaps some of you feel like that, or know someone in your family like it.

A week after the disciples had told Thomas that they had seen Jesus alive, and he had said, 'Unless I see the nail marks in his hands and put my finger where the nails were, and put my hand into his side, I will not believe it', Thomas went with the other disciples to pray and eat together. Suddenly, there was Jesus standing with them, large as life and obviously completely alive! 'Hello!' he said. 'Peace be with you!' That's what people always said to each other when they met. (They can try greeting each other like this.)

Now for our next question: 'Jesus will ignore Thomas because Thomas hadn't believed that he was alive.' How likely is that? (Use the chart again.) Well, we are told that what happened was this. Jesus went straight across to Thomas, and said, 'Put your finger here. See my hands. Reach out your hand and put it into my side. Stop doubting and believe.' (Have this written large on another speech bubble.) So what will Thomas do now, do you think?

Last question: 'Thomas will only believe when he has touched Jesus' wounds to make certain it's true.' How likely is that? (Use the chart for their ideas.) Well, in fact Thomas found he didn't need to do all that. Just knowing Jesus was there was enough for him, and this time, instead of saying, 'Unless I see the nail marks in his hands and put my finger where the nails were, and put my hand into his side, I will not believe it', he said, 'My Lord and my God!' (Another speech bubble.) Jesus was very glad that Thomas now knew he was alive, and would be alive for ever. And he thought of all the people who would still believe even though they couldn't actually see him. I'm looking at some of those people now! Is there anyone here who knows that Jesus is alive, even though they haven't seen him? Well, Jesus was talking about you in that room nearly two thousand years ago. And this is what he said: 'Blessed are those who have not seen and yet have believed.' (Last speech bubble.) That's us!

Praying

Use the prayer on the worksheet.

Activities

Following the instructions on the sheet, the children can make a kite which can fly in the invisible wind. Each child will need a plastic bag and some wool or thin string, and various decorative stickers.

How does your life show that Jesus is alive?

So is the wind really there when the kite flies?

If the wind isn't blowing, what happens?

To pray this week

With my eyes I may not be able to see you, Jesus, but I know you are real and I know you are here. With my hands I may not be able to touch you, Jesus, but my heart feels your love, your peace and your strength.

FLY THE KITE IN THE WIND

What you do

1. Cut along the bottom of the bag

2. Wind some wire into a circle to fit this end of the bag

3. Roll the edges of the bag over the wire and fix with staples and tape

4. Do the same at the top of the bag, but keep the handles on

5. Decorate the kite

6. Tie a piece of string between the handles, threading the ring on to it

7. Tie the rest of the string on to one side of the ring

8. Let it go, but hold on to the end of the string!

You will need

plastic bag

light, thin wire

a curtain ring

string

paints and stickers

sticky tape

stapler

THIRD SUNDAY OF EASTER

Thought for the day

Jesus explains the scriptures and is recognised in the breaking of bread.

Readings

Acts 2:14a, 36-41
Psalm 116:1-4, 12-19
1 Peter 1:17-23
Luke 24:13-35

Aim

To know what happened on the road to Emmaus and the effect it had on the two disciples.

Starter

AA road map. Sit the children in a circle and label them (only verbally) in order, so that everyone is called one of three or four local roads. If you wish, you can include 'Emmaus Road'. When you call out a particular road name, those with that name have to change places. If you call 'AA road map!' everyone changes places.

Teaching

Ideally you will be taking the children out on a short walk as part of today's teaching, provided this is safe and practical, and there are sufficient adult helpers. If you can take them out, plan a route where you can move from Jerusalem to Emmaus and back; for instance, if Jerusalem is in the church hall, Emmaus might be the church porch, or the vicarage garden. If an outside journey is not practical, then make your Jerusalem and Emmaus within the teaching area, but as far from each other as possible. Gather the children in Jerusalem.

Since Easter we have been looking at how Jesus' friends discovered that he wasn't dead any more, but very much alive. Today's story takes place along a road – the road between Jerusalem and Emmaus. Luke was told this story by someone called Cleophas, who remembered all the details for ever afterwards, because he and his wife or friend – we don't know which – had never been so surprised as they were that day. We are going to walk where these two friends of Jesus walked, and find out what happened.

Explain that the two disciples were very sad that day because Jesus was dead and they missed him. They were also very confused and disappointed, because they had great hopes for Jesus being a national leader; they'd even thought he was the promised Messiah, but presumed they must have got it all wrong. They started off for home, which was seven miles from Jerusalem.

At this point gather everyone up and walk slowly along as you tell the next part of the story. Have one of the leaders who has been absent up till now join the group. This person takes up the story, from the point where Jesus joins them, and explains how the stranger helped the disciples to understand some of the prophecies from the scriptures which suggested that the Messiah would actually have to suffer and die in order to save his people, but that he would rise again.

By this time you will be approaching Emmaus. The first leader takes over the story, about the disciples inviting the stranger in, when he is making as if to go on, and the group goes into the Emmaus 'home'. The leaders produce some bread as they talk about the disciples having a meal together with the stranger. The second leader takes the bread and begins to break it while telling the children what the stranger did. The disciples suddenly realise who this stranger is – they recognise that he is Jesus, fully alive! During the excitement of this discovery, and the children guessing, the second leader discreetly leaves, and then the first leader tells how Jesus vanished once the disciples have realised who he is. They are really happy and decide to go straight back all the way to Jerusalem. (How far was it?) So everyone runs back to Jerusalem to tell the disciples there that they now know Jesus is alive – they've just met him!

Praying

The children can say this prayer as they walk along, perhaps with everyone walking round in a circle as at a skating rink. The leader can be one of the children.

Leader	Walk with me, Jesus.
All	Walk with me, Jesus.
Leader	Show me the way.
All	Show me the way.
Leader	Walk with me, Jesus.
All	Walk with me, Jesus.
Leader	Every day.
All	Every day.

Activities

On the sheet the teaching is reinforced with a puzzle path, and the children are encouraged to think about areas in their lives where they specially want to ask Jesus to walk with them and their friends.

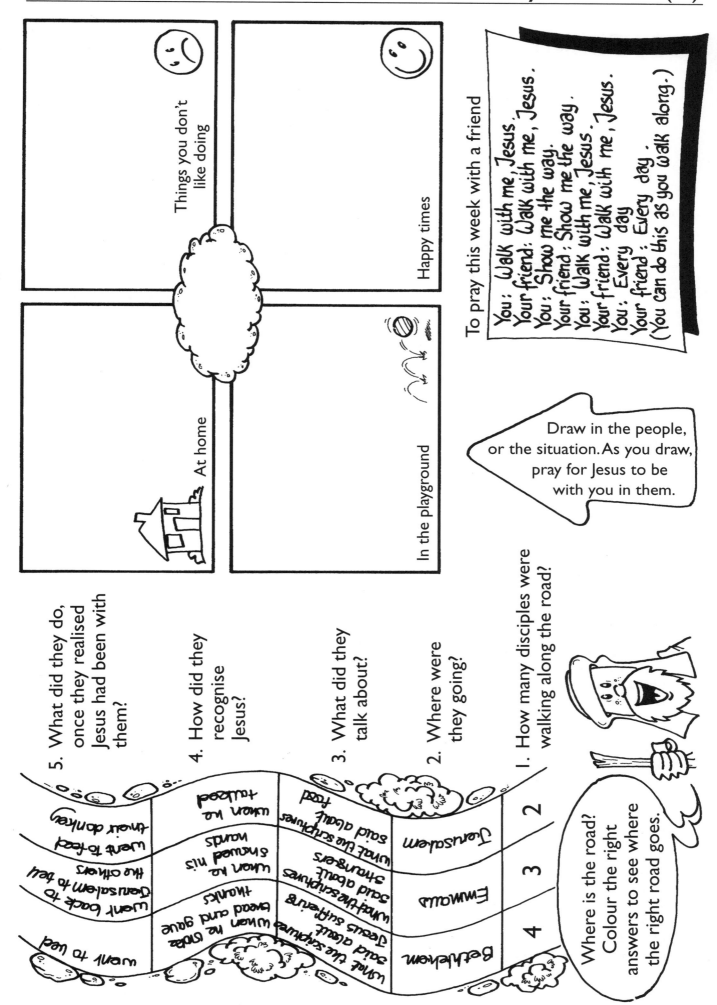

Things you don't like doing

Happy times

At home

In the playground

To pray this week with a friend

You: Walk with me, Jesus.
Your friend: Walk with me, Jesus.
You: Show me the way.
Your friend: Show me the way.
You: Walk with me, Jesus.
Your friend: Walk with me, Jesus.
You: Every day.
Your friend: Every day.
(You can do this as you walk along.)

Draw in the people, or the situation. As you draw, pray for Jesus to be with you in them.

5. What did they do, once they realised Jesus had been with them?

4. How did they recognise Jesus?

3. What did they talk about?

2. Where were they going?

1. How many disciples were walking along the road?

Where is the road? Colour the right answers to see where the right road goes.

FOURTH SUNDAY OF EASTER

Thought for the day

Jesus, the Good Shepherd, has come so that we may have life in rich abundance.

Readings

Acts 2:42-47
Psalm 23
1 Peter 2:19-25
John 10:1-10

Aim

To look at what Jesus meant by saying he was the Good Shepherd, and the sheep door.

Starter

Give everyone a paper sheep to cut out and write their name on, and stick them all on a pre-painted hilly background with a shepherd standing in the middle.

Teaching

Display the sheep picture and start writing the words to go underneath it, one by one: *The Lord is my shepherd*. As you write the first word the children repeat it, catching hold of the thumb of their left hand. With the second word they catch hold of their index finger and so on. Soon they will have learnt the whole sentence. Now point out that each of the sheep on the picture has a particular name. If we are all those sheep, who do they think the shepherd is? It's Jesus. Jesus called himself the Good Shepherd because he looks after his sheep (that's us). Go through the sentence again, hanging on to your ring fingers as you emphasise that the Lord is *my* shepherd – and that means John's, Abigail's, Thomas's and Ali's shepherd.

We all need food and drink, shelter and sleep, of course, but we are not just bodies, so it is not just our bodies that need feeding and looking after. Our spirit is the real us that lives in our body, and that part of us is what goes on living in heaven after our body has died.

When Jesus said he was like a shepherd to us, he was talking about looking after those spirits of ours. (Place a jagged sign called 'Sin' on the floor.) Jesus knows that bad and wrong ideas come to us sometimes in life, like attacking wolves, and he says he will fight off those evils to keep our bodies and spirits safe, if only we will let him. (Place a cross to 'cross out' the sin.)

(Place an open Bible and bread and wine on the floor.) Our spirits need feeding, like our bodies, and Jesus will feed us with God's words of love and wise help, often through our Bible reading, at Living Stones, through the bread and wine at Communion, in the beauty of the world and through other people we meet.

(Place a compass on the floor.) Our spirits need guiding and teaching, and Jesus will whisper into our hearts the sense of what is right and wrong, so that we know, and can choose the best direction to go in.

(Place a phone on the floor.) Our spirits need friendship, and Jesus gives us that, too. We can talk with him about anything, anywhere, and be sure that he is interested, and has time to listen to us. And he gives us the company and friendship of other Christians to help us as well, which is very important.

Praying

The Lord is my shepherd;
I have everything I need.
He gives me rest in green pastures.
He leads me to calm water.
He gives me new strength.
For the good of his name,
he leads me on paths that are right.
Even if I walk through the dark valley of death,
I will not be afraid because you are with me.
Your rod and your staff comfort me.

(From Psalm 23)

Activities

On the activity sheet there are instructions for making today's prayer into a stand-up card in the shape of a sheep. The children can either use the shape drawn on the sheet or you can make thin card templates from this beforehand, and they can draw round these on to coloured card. There is also a code to crack for which they will need to refer to a Bible.

Notes

Jesus said
(JOHN 10:10)

'The Lord is my shepherd, I have everything I need'

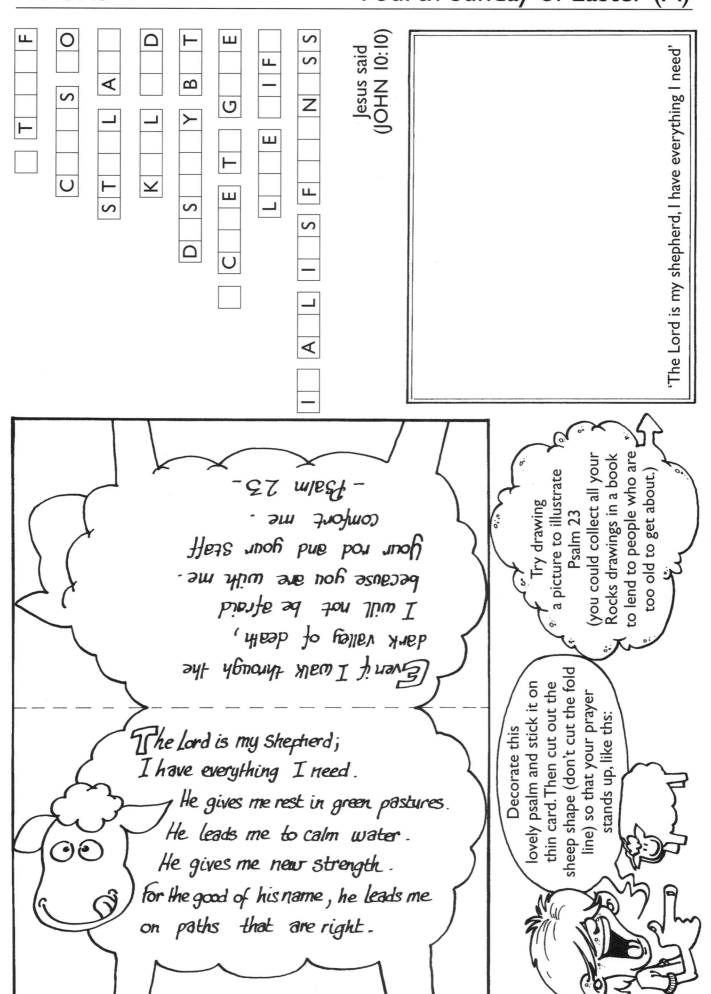

The Lord is my shepherd;
I have everything I need.
He gives me rest in green pastures.
He leads me to calm water.
He gives me new strength.
For the good of his name, he leads me
on paths that are right.

Even if I walk through the
dark valley of death,
I will not be afraid
because you are with me -
your rod and your staff
comfort me -
– Psalm 23 –

Try drawing
a picture to illustrate
Psalm 23
(you could collect all your
Rocks drawings in a book
to lend to people who are
too old to get about.)

Decorate this
lovely psalm and stick it on
thin card. Then cut out the
sheep shape (don't cut the fold
line) so that your prayer
stands up, like this:

FIFTH SUNDAY OF EASTER

Thought for the day

Jesus is the Way, the Truth and the Life, through whom we can come into the presence of God for ever.

Readings

Acts 7:55-60
Psalm 31:1-5, 15-16
1 Peter 2:2-10
John 14:1-14

Aim

To explore what it means to look at Jesus as the Way, the Truth and the Life.

Starter

Set up a narrow way to walk along. (It might be a thin strip of card, or two skipping ropes, laid on the floor.) Everyone can try walking along it without falling off and being caught by all the alligators (those who are not walking along the thin road!). If they are caught by an alligator (touching is quite enough) they are out. Alligators are not allowed to get them while they are on the road.

Teaching

Bring along some newspaper pictures and headlines which tell of war and sad things, and introduce them, one by one, before dotting them around on the floor in the centre of the circle. Talk with them about there being so many sad and bad and dangerous things in this life, as well as all that is lovely and good. It is important for us on our Christian journey to know that this is true. There are lots of things to tempt us into doing wrong and unkind and selfish things. It is not easy to walk through life doing what is right.

Read together what Jesus says about all this: 'Don't let your hearts be troubled. Trust in God and trust in me . . . You know the way to the place where I am going.' Thomas said to Jesus, 'Lord, we don't know where you are going. So how can we know the way?'

Now take a length of string and wind it on a safe way between all the pictures and headlines, right across the circle, as someone reads the next sentence: 'Jesus answered, "I am the Way. And I am the Truth and the Life. The only way to the Father is through me."' Explain that Jesus was saying that he is like the safe path through a minefield; his close friendship with us all through our life is like a clear road for us to walk along to heaven. Give out separate words of 'I am the Way, the Truth and the Life' to different children and let them lay these words in order along the winding string 'road'. Then everyone can say them together.

Praying

Jesus, I know that you are the Way,
the Truth and the Life.
Let me walk safely each day
through all the troubles and temptations
by walking your Way
which leads me to heaven. Amen.

Activities

Today's teaching is reinforced and developed in the activity sheet with situations to think about which will help them see where the Jesus Way lies, and there is a compass to make to sense Jesus' directing in each situation. If you want to, you could adapt this and give each child a real compass to stick on the centre – that depends on your numbers and your budget!

Notes

WHICH WAY?!

START

Your friend is ill in hospital.

Do nothing → This is unkind. If you treat your friends like that you need to change. Try again.

Visit/send a card → Now you can't find your lunch box.

Tell the truth → Now you need a ball and yours is flat.

Take someone else's ball → This is stealing and stealing is wrong and unloving. Try again.

Pretend someone stole it → This is dishonest. You need to get brave and tell the truth. Try again.

play something that doesn't need a ball → Now your parents ask you to help tidy up.

You don't do it → This is selfish. You need to learn to help others even when you don't want to. Try again.

You do it → Now someone is making you upset and angry.

You hit them → This is letting your anger be in control. You need to be in control of your temper. Try again.

You explain and go away to cool down → Well done!

How to make a compass

You will need

an iron nail

a magnet

What you do

1. Stroke the nail with the magnet, always going the same way, like this: (lift the magnet high over the nail on the way back each time)

2. Lay the magnetised nail on the paper

3. Lay the paper in a bowl of water. The nail will turn the paper so it points to North

---

Colour and cut out

N

NW NE

W E

SW SE

S

NORTH SOUTH EAST WEST

WHICH WAY IS BEST!

THE JESUS WAY

To pray this week

Jesus, I know that you are the Way, the Truth and the Life. Let me walk safely each day through all the troubles and temptations by walking your Way which leads me to heaven.
— Amen —

Sixth Sunday of Easter

Thought for the day

The Spirit of truth, given to us, enables us to discern the living, risen Christ.

Readings

Acts 17:22-31
Psalm 66:8-20
1 Peter 3:13-22
John 14:15-21

Aim

To see obedience as a mark of love.

Starter

Square bashing. First teach the children how to stand to attention, to stand at ease, to about-turn right and left, and to march. Then line them up like an army and be a sergeant major, taking them through their paces.

Teaching

Explain how, in the army (or navy or air force), everyone has to obey orders, and drill like that helps the soldiers get used to doing what they are told straight away. It just wouldn't work, where there are guns and explosives around, to have people who were not disciplined; obedience is a matter of life or death.

Most of us find it hard to be obedient – we would rather do what we want than what we are told! But Jesus can't use us as his soldiers in the battle against evil unless we are trained to obey him, like good soldiers obey their commanders. Jesus told his followers this: 'If you love me, you will do the things I command. The one who knows my commands and obeys them is the one who loves me.'

Jesus isn't getting hold of us in a half-Nelson and saying, 'Now listen you, obey me or else!' He would never, ever want to force us to do anything. He respects us too much for that. But he *is* saying, 'OK, you say that you love me and trust me as your Lord. If you really meant that, you would be doing what I told you, out of love and respect for me. If you just go on pleasing yourself, and doing what you want all the time, it shows that you don't really love me at all.'

He's right, and we can't get away from it. If we do mean it when we say we love and trust Jesus, then we'll have to get in training to be more obedient. At our Baptism this was said to us: 'Fight valiantly under the banner of Christ against sin, the world and the devil, and continue his faithful soldier and servant to the end of your life.'

There's a very helpful song for today called *To be with you* by Mike Burn which is recorded (*Kids' Praise, 96*), so you could sing and dance along to it. Otherwise, finish with a couple of swiftly obeyed marching commands.

Praying

(To be said while marching on the spot.)

I love to be with you, Jesus,
so I'm going to do as you say,
I'll show that I love you and want to be like you
by doing your will TODAY.

(End by jumping to attention.)

Activities

On the sheet there are instructions for making an arm-band badge which says 'God's soldier in training'. The children will each need a strip of material (cut from an old sheet or shirt, perhaps) long enough to tie round their upper arm. There are also examples of ways God can use our obedience.

Notes

How can God use obedient soldiers like us?

WASH HERE
CAR?

Help us pay for a clean well for this village

To do important jobs

To be faithful in prayer

To help someone calm down

Who's soldiers are we?
WE'RE SOLDIERS OF OUR GOD!

What war are we fighting?
WE'RE FIGHTING EVIL AND SIN!

What have we got to protect us?
WE'VE GOT THE ARMOUR OF GOD!

I'll help you with it — then we'll play later

To support others in good living

I'm afraid it was me, sir

To stand up for what is right

3. Ask a friend to tie the band round the top part of your arm (not too tight!)

4. You can wear it while you say the marching prayer again, or this chant

Hang on, I'm still making it!

Got your arm badge yet?

You will need

a strip of material

felt-tip pens

1. Write in black pen:
GOD'S SOLDIER IN TRAINING
(Leaders write it on first in pencil

2. Decorate with coloured pens

To pray this week

(a marching prayer on the spot)
I love to be with you, Jesus,
so I'm going to do as you say,
I'll show that I love you
and want to be like you
by doing your will
TODAY!
(Jump to attention)

ASCENSION DAY

Thought for the day

Having bought back our freedom with the giving of his life, Jesus enters into the full glory to which he is entitled.

Readings

Acts 1:1-11 or Daniel 7:9-14
Psalm 47 or Psalm 93
Ephesians 1:15-23 or Acts 1:1-11
Luke 24:44-53

Activities

It is likely that Ascension Day services for schools will not need a separate programme for children and young people. Children in church can work on this drawing and colouring activity during the sermon.

SEVENTH SUNDAY OF EASTER

Thought for the day

God's glory is often revealed in the context of suffering and failure in the world's eyes.

Readings

Acts 1:6-14
Psalm 68:1-10, 32-35
1 Peter 4:12-14; 5:6-11
John 17:1-11

Aim

To see the Ascension in the context of the Resurrection and the coming of the Holy Spirit.

Starter

Cut several series of pictures from comic strips and fix them in groups on the walls, in random order. The children walk around the room on their own or with a friend or two, sorting the pictures into the right sequence. You can then take each group of pictures down in turn and put them in the correct order so everyone can check it against their own ideas.

Teaching

Using one of the sets of pictures, get the children to explain why one picture couldn't possibly come before another. We have been picking up the clues based on what we know – a cat can't get wet before it has fallen into the water; a rocket cannot be in a thousand pieces before it has exploded. Today we are going to look at the order of events after Jesus' death, and see why they had to be in that order.

First there had to be the cross. (Place a cross on the floor at one end of the room.) It was through dying for us that Jesus set us free. This is how he saved the world with love. (Unwind a ball of string, starting at the cross, and taking it across the floor to a message which says, 'Jesus is alive!') Being the Lord of Life, death simply could not hold him prisoner for long, so the next thing for Jesus the Son of God had to be the Resurrection on Easter Day. (Unwind the string further, and place some broken bread on a plate on the floor.) Jesus needed his friends to know that he really was alive, so he appeared to them at different times, and often it was when he broke the bread that they recognised him. (Unwind the string a bit more, and place down a cut-out cloud.)

Once the disciples had begun to realise that Jesus could be with them without having to be seen all the time, they were ready for the next stage. Jesus had promised his disciples that he was on his way back to the Father, but that he wouldn't leave them on their own. Once he had returned to heaven they would be able to receive the power of the Holy Spirit. Jesus first had to go in glory back into heaven, so that (unwind more string to a picture of tongues of flames) the disciples could receive that power of the Holy Spirit.

Place a Bible, open at the Acts 1 reading, next to the cloud. Explain that this is how Luke tells us what happened on the day when Jesus was taken up into the glory of heaven. Read the account, using a version of the text accessible to children.

Praying

Jesus, you are our Lord and Saviour,
reigning in the glory of heaven!
You were sent to love us to freedom
and you did it!
Glory to you for ever.

Activities

On the sheet there is a picture of the Ascension for them to complete, and a wordsearch to help reinforce the Easter season vocabulary. They can also create their own picture(s) of how they imagine it might have been in heaven as Jesus appeared, with all the angels cheering and praising God for the great victory.

Notes

Can you draw in what the disciples are looking at as they stare upwards

To pray this week

Jesus, you are our lord and Saviour
reigning in the glory of heaven!
You were sent to love us
to freedom
and you did it!
Glory to you for ever.

WORD SEARCH

C	R	O	S	S	G	O	O	D	A
R	A	I	O	T	Q	H	M	F	S
U	S	N	S	A	V	E	D	R	C
C	X	Z	B	E	U	A	T	I	E
I	Y	R	J	A	N	V	I	D	N
F	L	Y	P	S	D	E	R	A	S
I	O	C	W	T	G	N	I	Y	I
E	H	B	R	E	A	D	P	F	O
D	L	I	E	R	H	K	S	V	N
R	E	C	O	G	N	I	S	E	D

**GOOD FRIDAY EASTER RISEN
ASCENSION HEAVEN BREAD
CRUCIFIED CROSS RECOGNISED
HOLY SPIRIT SAVED**

Pentecost

Thought for the day

With great power the Spirit of God is poured out on the expectant disciples.

Readings

Acts 2:1-21 or Numbers 11:24-30
Psalm 104:24-34, 35b
1 Corinthians 12:3b-13 or Acts 2:1-21
John 20:19-23 or John 7:37-39

Aim

To know the Pentecost story.

Starter

Using red, orange and yellow crepe paper, cut strips and bunch some of these strips together to make cheerleader streamers, like this:

Teaching

First practise making a collective sound of wind, not by blowing, but breathing out with mouths open. Try it quietly at first, and then much more loudly. We are going to hear about the day when God breathed his life and power into his people.

First go round noisily shutting windows and doors, and turning keys in locks, as you tell the children how the disciples were gathered as usual to pray. Just over a week ago they had seen Jesus taken up into heaven, and had been told to wait in Jerusalem for the coming of the Holy Spirit. They had no idea what that meant, or what to expect, but Jesus had told them to wait expectantly, so that is what they would do.

Now play some quiet music (*Waiting for your Spirit* springs to mind, but any quiet worship music would be suitable). Suggest we all sit waiting for God, as those disciples did that morning, waiting for God to give us the gift of his Spirit.

Suddenly there was a sound, like this (all start the quiet out-breathing), rather like wind, coming from the sky and getting closer. It was the sound of God, breathing his Holy Spirit into his loyal friends. The sound got louder (all breathe out more loudly), until the whole house they were in seemed surrounded by the living, moving presence of almighty God. (Everyone picks up their streamers and shakers, stands up and whirls them round about as you tell the next part of the story.) Now it was as if tongues of flame flickered out from the breath of God and found each person, resting on them very gently. (The streamers are brought gently down to rest on the floor between the children.)

The disciples were all filled with God's Holy Spirit, and they started praising God and shouting out their love for him. They didn't care what anyone else thought of them, their love for God bubbled up inside them and all they wanted to do was thank him and tell him their love. They lifted their hands and all started talking at once. (Put on a praise tape which they know really well, such as *I reach up high*, so they can all dance and sing their hearts out to their God, waving their streamers.)

Quite a crowd had gathered outside the house, wondering what was going on so early in the morning. Still full of God's Spirit, the disciples ran out to share the good news. That's what the Church, including us, has been called to do ever since – to be filled with God's living Spirit, and in our excitement and joy, run out to share the good news with all the people we meet.

Praying

Breathe on me, too, Lord God almighty,
as you breathed on the disciples that day.
Touch me with your fire
and set me ablaze with your love!

Activities

Have some red, orange and yellow pieces of tissue, out of which the children can cut flame shapes to stick on the headband and make a hat of flame. There are also flame shapes on the sheet with space for them to write on the message of God's love they want people to know. They can colour these, cut them out and give them to people.

> *Notes*

Cut along here

Touch me with your fire and
set me ablaze with your love!

Ideas for messages . . .

Live in the Spirit of God

May God's love give you joy

May you know the power of God's love

Peace be with you

God loves you

May the Holy Spirit fill your life

To pray this week

Breathe on me, too, Lord God almighty, as you breathed on the disciples that day. Touch me with your fire and set me ablaze with your love!

Colour the flames and write messages on them. Give them to people in church or to someone you pray for.

Cut out flames from coloured tissue and stick them on the head band. Fix the head band to fit with staples or glue or sticky tape.

ORDINARY TIME

TRINITY SUNDAY

Thought for the day

The mystery of God – Creator, Redeemer and Sanctifier all at once – is beyond our human understanding, yet closer to us than breathing.

Readings

Isaiah 40:12-17, 27-31
Psalm 8
2 Corinthians 13:11-13
Matthew 28:16-20

Aim

To start exploring how God is one God, yet community.

Starter

Play a game where teams are involved. Depending on your group this could be a ball game, or a party team game, such as 'flip the kipper' (each team member waving a newspaper fish along a course using sheets of newspaper).

Teaching

In a large bowl have a jug full of water, and a small cup. Tell everyone we are going to stage an experiment today. We are going to see if all the water in the jug will fit into the cup. Try this and discover that it won't. Why not? There was too much water for the little cup to cope with all at once.

Ask them to imagine that the little cup is a human mind, and all the water, not just in a jug, but in all the seas and oceans and rivers and clouds, is like God. There is far more to God than we, with our little cup-sized human minds, can possibly cope with or understand. But then, if God was just another little cup like us, why on earth would we worship him? We worship God because he is the source, or beginning and the end of all things, because he is the great power behind all life and existence, and because he is the one true God, altogether too great and full of mystery for us to ever understand.

The amazing thing is that this God, full of mystery, has got time for us! He actually knows everything about each person in this room, each person in church, each person in this town and this country, and each person in every country of the whole world. Not just those alive now, but all the ones who have ever lived and who will ever live. And

that's pretty impressive. And what's more, he was willing to come and live among us as a human person, called Jesus, and through the Holy Spirit he is alive in human people of every time and place, when they put their trust in him.

We find ourselves saying, 'But how can God be One God when we talk about him as the Father, Jesus and the Holy Spirit? Isn't that three, rather than one?' Well, no, it isn't three Gods, it's all One God, but it is three persons united and co-operating in the one God, which we call TRI (=3) + UNITY (=1) = TRINITY. Yes, it's impossible for us to understand. That doesn't mean it can't be true, though; it means that God is truly the greatest, and far greater than a human mind.

Praying

Holy God, greater than our knowing,
we worship you.
Holy God, more than we can understand,
we worship you.
Holy God, knowing all things,
yet loving each of us,
we worship you.

Activities

Traditionally, the Trinity colour is green. Stick green wool on to the Celtic Trinity pattern on the sheet, to help everyone sense the way God is three in unity and co-operation, without beginning or end. There are also examples of things they are trying to understand and others they may understand some day but would never be able to fully explain.

Notes

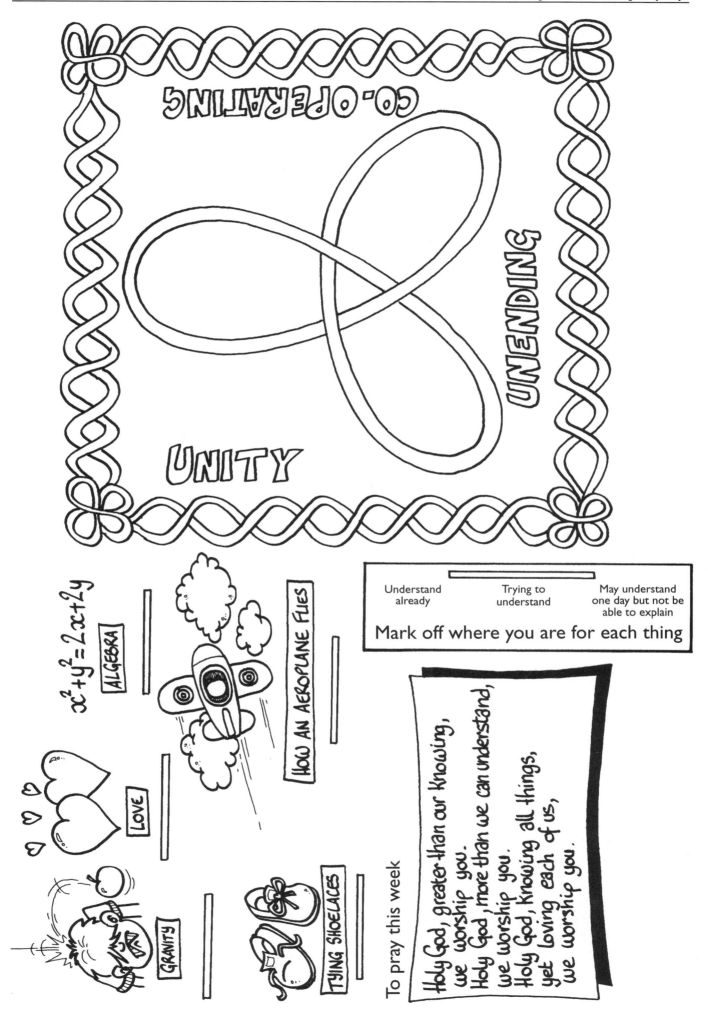

CO-OPERATING

UNENDING

UNITY

$x^2 + y^2 = 2x + 2y$ ALGEBRA

HOW AN AEROPLANE FLIES

LOVE

GRAVITY

TYING SHOELACES

| Understand already | Trying to understand | May understand one day but not be able to explain |

Mark off where you are for each thing

To pray this week

Holy God, greater than our knowing,
we worship you.
Holy God, more than we can understand,
we worship you.
Holy God, knowing all things,
yet loving each of us,
we worship you.

PROPER 4

Sunday between 29 May and 4 June inclusive
(if after Trinity Sunday)

Thought for the day

Wise listeners build their lives up on the strong rock of the word of God.

Readings

Deuteronomy 11:18-21, 26-28; Psalm 31:1-5, 19-24
Romans 1:16-17; 3:22b-28 (29-31); Matthew 7:21-29

Aim

To think about the need to change words into a way of life.

Starter

Divide the group into teams and have a set of instructions for each team. Each team is given their first instruction which they rush off and do, bringing back the answer before you give them the next instruction. The first team to complete all their instructions wins. Here are some suggestions for the instructions; you will need to vary them according to the size and age of the teams and the practicalities of your meeting area.

- Bring a list of signatures of everyone in the team.
- Make a thumb-print pattern using everyone's thumbs.
- Collect six different coloured pieces of wool from around the room.
- How far from the wall do you stretch if you all lie end to end?
- Stand in order of height/hair length.
- Bring the total number of fingers and toes in the team.

Teaching

Draw attention to the way they needed to do two things in that game:

1. To listen carefully to what they were told.
2. To carry out the instructions.

Praise them for doing that really well, working with each other and helping one another. That's very much what Jesus was teaching – he could have used our Rocks in Living Stones as an example to the people of how to listen carefully and then put what we hear into action!

Anyone who goes to dancing, or sports training, or is learning to play a musical instrument will know that the way to do it is to listen to what your teacher or trainer says, and then do your practice.

As you put into practice what you have been taught, you find yourself getting better and better. When you listen, and then don't get round to practising, you don't make nearly as much progress.

Jesus is our trainer and teacher, who tells us all about living. One day he was getting rather fed up with people coming to listen to him and saying they were his followers, even though they weren't changing their lives at all. And this is what he said to them: 'Not everyone who says that I am his Lord will enter the kingdom of heaven. The only people who will enter the kingdom of heaven are those who *do* the things that my Father in heaven wants.' It just isn't enough to say that we are followers of Jesus – if we really mean that, we will make sure we put into practice what he tells us.

Then Jesus told one of his stories to help the people understand what he was saying. He said that the people who hear what he says and then act on it are like wise builders, who build their house on proper foundations of solid rock. (Build a brick house on a firm but well-protected surface as you speak.) Those who hear what Jesus tells them and yet do nothing about it are as foolish as builders who build their house on sand. (Build another house on a tray of dry sand.)

What is so wise about building on rock? When the storms of life pour down it will still stay standing. (Pour water over the house on rock.) When the storms of life pour down on a house built on sand, it's a different story completely. (Pour water over the sand so that the house built on it collapses.)

So the wise thing for us to do is not just to hear what Jesus says, or even to hear and say, 'Oh yes, I'm a follower of Jesus – he's my Lord!' The wise thing is actually to do something about what he tells us – to start putting his teaching into action so that our lives and behaviour are like strong houses built on strong foundations.

They can sing *The wise man built his house upon the rock* (CHB) with actions of building (fist on fist), rain coming down (wiggling fingers moving down) and floods coming up (hands sweeping upwards).

Praying

Lord Jesus, I want to be a real follower of yours.
I don't just want to say it,
I want to do it as well.
Please help me to put what you tell me
into practice this week. Amen.

Activities

On the sheet there are Deuteronomy-style reminders to make and strap on to themselves with bracelets and headbands, and fridge magnets and mirror messages to fix around the house. The children will need a blob of blutack each, or a small piece of magnetic strip (available from craft shops).

PROPER 5

Sunday between 5 and 11 June inclusive
(if after Trinity Sunday)

Thought for the day

Jesus' life of healing and compassion acts out God's desire for mercy rather than empty sacrifice.

Readings

Hosea 5:15-6:6
Psalm 50:7-15
Romans 4:13-25
Matthew 9:9-13, 18-26

Aim

To know about our calling to show mercy in our lives and be real in our worship.

Starter

Lying. Sit in a circle. The first person mimes an action (such as brushing their teeth) and everyone else joins in the mime. The person next to them says, 'What are you doing?' to which the first person lies, 'I'm blowing my nose' (or anything else that they aren't actually miming), and everyone says, 'I'm blowing my nose', while they continue to mime brushing their teeth. Then it's the next person's turn to start a mime.

Teaching

In that game they were saying one thing and doing another. That's just fine in a game, but today we're looking at what can happen if people say one thing when they're talking to God, but do something quite different in their lives.

Tell the children to put both thumbs up each time they think something sounds good, and down if they think it sounds bad.

It all started with Jesus making some friends. (This is a thumbs up.) These friends led bad lives, cheating people of money, and working for the Romans. (Thumbs down.) One of these friends was called Matthew, and Jesus called Matthew to follow him and be one of his disciples. (Thumbs up.) Matthew was very pleased to be asked (thumbs up) and threw a party for all his friends to celebrate. (Thumbs up.) There was lots to eat and drink (thumbs up), and Jesus and his friends were really enjoying themselves. (Thumbs up.)

The Pharisees, who were the religious leaders, saw Jesus enjoying himself with these bad people and they were angry. (Thumbs down.) They went up to Jesus' followers to complain. (Thumbs down.) 'What does Jesus think he's doing, spending his time with these kinds of people?' they said. 'They are bad people, and it isn't right for a religious teacher to waste his time with bad people. He should have nothing to do with them!' (Thumbs down.)

Jesus heard what they were saying and came over to talk with them. (Thumbs up.) He wanted them to understand that God loves all people, whether they are bad or good. (Thumbs up.) He wanted them to see that he was giving these people the love and healing they needed. (Thumbs up.) So he decided to give the Pharisees a clue. He said to them: 'Healthy people don't need a doctor. Only the sick need a doctor.' He hoped this would help them see that what he was doing was good, not bad; that it was not against God's way, but was exactly what God would want. (Thumbs up.)

But the Pharisees did not understand. (Thumbs down.) Although in their worship they said they loved God (one thumb up) here they were being angry at Jesus for showing the love of God to these people who needed it (other thumb down). They were saying good things to God in their worship (one thumb up), but thinking bad things about God in their lives (other thumb down).

Jesus told them to go and sort out what was really important to God – saying you love him but not showing love to other people (thumbs down) or saying you love him and showing that by loving those he has made (thumbs up).

Praying

I want to worship the real, living God.
And I want my worship to be
not just an empty shell
but real.

Activities

On the sheet there are instructions for using a hard-boiled egg to reinforce today's teaching. Each child will need a hard-boiled egg, salt, pepper and mayonnaise, a spoon and a clean empty yoghurt pot. There is also a picture of Jesus at Matthew's party for them to add the Pharisees and colour.

Notes

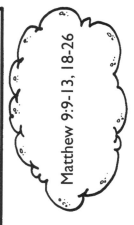

MATTHEW'S PARTY
The artist has forgotten some of the guests. Can you draw them in?
Guests: Jesus, tax collectors, sinners, Pharisees. Show what they are thinking.

Matthew 9:9-13, 18-26

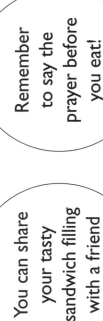

Remember to say the prayer before you eat!

You can share your tasty sandwich filling with a friend

To pray this week

I want to worship the real, living God. And I want my worship to be not just an empty shell but real.

NOT JUST AN EMPTY SHELL!

1. Tap the shell till it cracks all over

2. Peel off the shell

3. Put your egg in your pot and chop it up with a knife or a pair of clean scissors

4. Add a little salt and pepper and a dessert-spoon of mayonnaise

5. Mix everything together well

6. Cover the pot with cling film

PROPER 6

Sunday between 12 and 18 June inclusive
(if after Trinity Sunday)

Thought for the day

Jesus sends his ambassadors out to proclaim God's kingdom and bring hope and peace of mind to the harassed and lost in every age.

Readings

Exodus 19:2-8a
Psalm 100
Romans 5:1-8
Matthew 9:35-10:8 (9-23)

Aim

To know the names of the disciples and why they were sent out at this stage.

Starter

Harvesters. Cut out lots of 'wheat', or scatter lots of long grass stalks all around the room. The idea is to see who can gather up most stalks between the starting and finishing whistle.

Teaching

They have just been gathering in the harvest, and, as with the real harvest, it's an urgent business, because you have to work hard to get all the harvest in before the winter storms begin. Where Jesus lived, in the area around Galilee, there were fields where the workers raced to get the harvest in each year. That's why Jesus used the harvest to explain the work his followers needed to be trained to do.

He could see that lots and lots of people were anxious and unhappy and discontented in their lives, and he wanted them all to know the happiness and hope of living at peace with God. They were a bit like all the wheat, ready and waiting to be gathered in to God's love. So Jesus said to his disciples, 'There are many people to harvest, but there are only a few workers to help harvest them. God owns the harvest. Pray to him that he will send more workers to help gather his harvest.' (Can they think of any harvest-workers they know who are spending their time gathering people into God's love?)

At that time Jesus had his little band of disciples, who he was training up for the job. (Lay twelve cards with their names on face down on the floor. On this side only the initial letter is written.) With a mixture of knowledge and guesswork, see how many correct ones they can uncover. Put these in one line and turn over the others, one at a time, with everyone saying the name, before turning it over again. Now try to remember what this group of names was. Carry on until they have managed to name all the disciples, and all the names are face up. Then read through the whole list, in whatever order you point to them. (This discourages some from going too fast for the others.)

Jesus sent these disciples out to all the surrounding villages and towns to tell people that the kingdom of God was very near, and to heal any who were ill. This was good training for when Jesus had returned to heaven, and it also meant the disciples were working as a team with Jesus. They were sent out without lots of personal comforts, or extra clothes, or heavy luggage, and were told not to take any food or money with them, but accept the food and shelter they were given, whatever it was like. That way the people would see that there was nothing in it for them, and they were doing it just out of love.

And that's how we need to live, when we are working with Jesus in God's harvest.

Praying

Dear Jesus, here I am, signing on.
I'd like to be a worker in your harvest.
I understand that the only pay
is the joy of knowing
that we are doing your will.
Use me, Lord!

Activities

Have twelve balloons so that the children can draw faces on them with acetate pens (protect clothing!) and fix name labels to them which they have copied from the sheet. These are in coded form to be worked out. There are also pictures of workers in the harvest, and suggestions of ways they, too, can join the team.

Notes

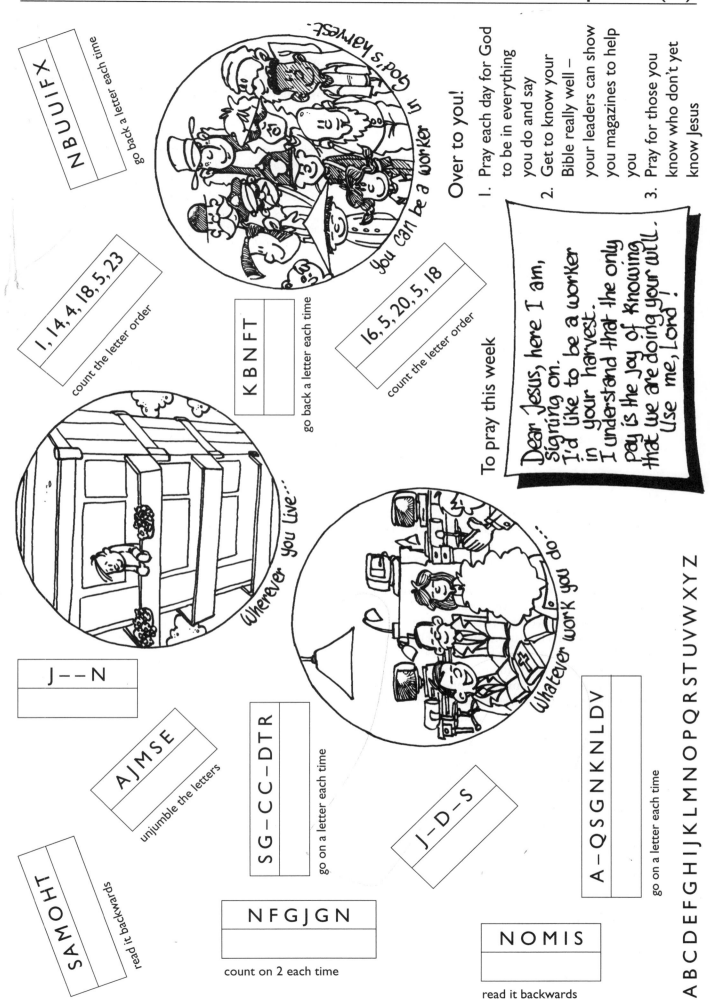

NBUUIFX
go back a letter each time

1, 14, 4, 18, 5, 23
count the letter order

KBNFT
go back a letter each time

16, 5, 20, 5, 18
count the letter order

You can be a worker in God's harvest.

Wherever you live...

Whatever work you do...

Over to you!

1. Pray each day for God to be in everything you do and say
2. Get to know your Bible really well – your leaders can show you magazines to help you
3. Pray for those you know who don't yet know Jesus

To pray this week

Dear Jesus, here I am, signing on. I'd like to be a worker in your harvest. I understand that the only pay is the joy of knowing that we are doing your will. Use me, Lord!

J – – N

AJMSE
unjumble the letters

SG – CC – DTR
go on a letter each time

SAMOHT
read it backwards

NFGJGN
count on 2 each time

J – D – S

A – QSGNKNLDV
go on a letter each time

NOMIS
read it backwards

A B C D E F G H I J K L M N O P Q R S T U V W X Y Z

Proper 7

Sunday between 19 and 25 June inclusive
(if after Trinity Sunday)

Thought for the day

When we are willing to take up our cross with Jesus we will also know his risen life.

Readings

Jeremiah 20:7-13
Psalm 69:7-10 (11-15) 16-18
Romans 6:1b-11
Matthew 10:24-39

Aim

To look at what it means to take up our cross and follow Jesus.

Starter

Follow my leader. The children can take it in turns to be leader, standing in front of everybody and doing various actions that are copied by the group.

Teaching

Show a number of crosses – one that hangs up, one on a neck chain, and a standing one, for instance, and gather from the children the reasons we Christians have a cross in our church and often in our home, and round our necks as well. What happened on a cross that we want to remember? Why is that so important to us? Draw out the fact that Jesus on the cross shows us that he was willing to die out of love for us, so that we could be freed to live as God planned for us, in close friendship with him.

When Jesus was teaching his disciples, he wanted them to know that following him would not always be easy. When we follow someone, we do what they have done. Jesus was willing to give up his life out of love for us. So true followers of Jesus will be the same. They will be so full of love for other people that they will be willing to give up their own selfishness. And that is what the shape of a cross is: a capital I crossed out. (Draw this for them as you say it.) Followers of Jesus do not put themselves first all the time; they think of the needs of other people. They don't push other people around or want everything their own way. Instead, because they love God and other people, they are happier working together with one another.

Jesus does not try and pretend that this will be easy, because he knows we all want to have our own way all the time, and if we are in the middle of a programme we really like, we don't want to stop and help someone else, or change channels so someone else in the family can watch their favourite film. It takes a long time to learn to cross out our selfishness, but the more we do it, Jesus says, the happier people we will become, and it will make God very happy, too.

Praying

Jesus, I know I am sometimes selfish.
  (draw a capital 'I')
Please help me to follow you closely,
crossing out the selfishness
  (cross through the 'I')
and living more lovingly.
  (look at the shape you have made)
Amen.

Activities

On the sheet they can draw their own large 'I' and then cross it out, as they say the prayer. There is also a coded puzzle to solve which leads them to Matthew 10:39, and some examples of different areas of possible selfishness to look at.

Notes

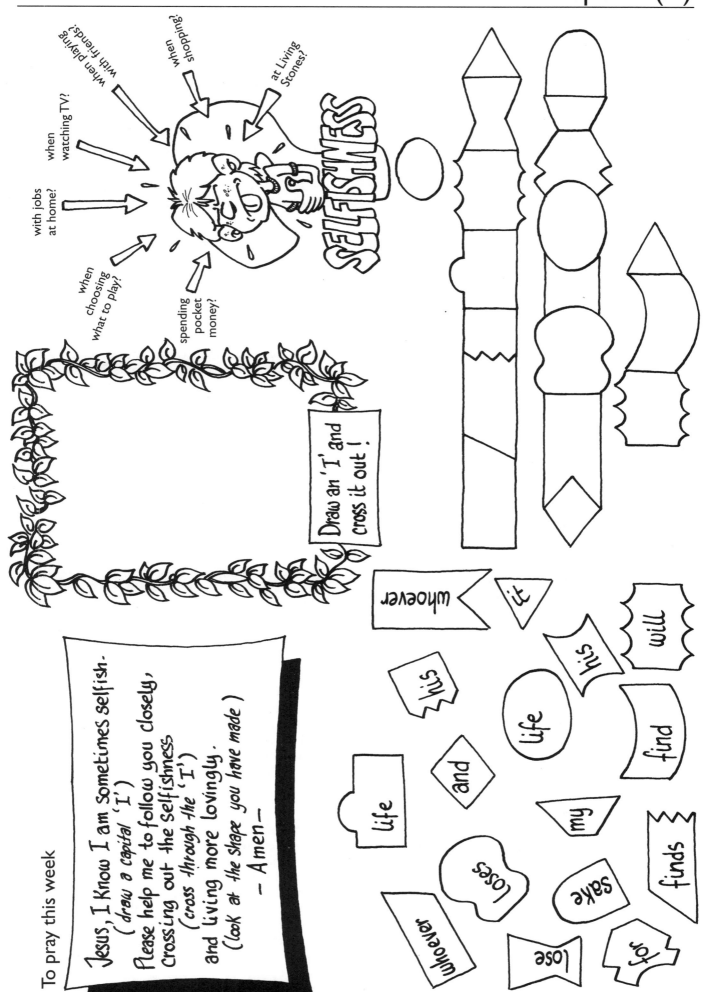

when playing with friends?

when shopping?

when watching TV?

at Living Stones?

with jobs at home?

when choosing what to play?

spending pocket money?

SELFISHNESS

Draw an 'I' and cross it out!

To pray this week

Jesus, I know I am sometimes selfish.
(draw a capital 'I')
Please help me to follow you closely,
crossing out the selfishness
(cross through the 'I')
and living more lovingly.
(look at the shape you have made)
— Amen —

whoever   it   his   will

his   life   find

and   my   finds

loses   sake

whoever   lose   for

Proper 8

Sunday between 26 June and 2 July inclusive

Thought for the day

As Christ's people we are no longer slaves to sin, but available for righteousness.

Readings

Jeremiah 28:5-9
Psalm 89:1-4, 15-18
Romans 6:12-23
Matthew 10:40-42

Aim

To learn about the difference between being slaves to sin and being free to do what is right out of thankful love.

Starter

Yes, your majesty! One of the leaders puts on a crown and robe, and holds a sceptre. (This can be a cracker hat, a curtain and a ruler.) She sits on her 'throne' and all the others are her slaves. She tells them what she wants done and everybody does it, first bowing down and saying, 'Yes, your majesty!' She might want to be fanned cool, given a can of drink, have it opened . . . and tested for poison, picked up, put down, or have a book brought and read and put away, or be scratched with a back-scratcher.

Teaching

Collect together some pictures from library books which show slaves building the pyramids, or rowing galleys, making bricks or harvesting sugar cane. When you are a slave someone pays money for you and then owns you, as if you are a bicycle or a TV. (You could act this out with one of the leaders being the buyer, and one of the children a person for sale.) As a slave you have to do what your owner tells you to do, and you don't belong to yourself any more. No one wants to be a slave, and even if you are lucky enough to have a kind owner, it's still hard to be owned like a thing, instead of being a free person, and slaves are often unhappy. It is not right for humans to be bought and owned like this.

Pin up a heading 'Slaves to sin'. When we are slaves to sin it is as if we are owned by sin, and spend our lives doing what our selfishness tells us to do. Give some examples of this, read by different children from speech bubbles of card:

- You want that big bit of cake, so take it quickly before anyone else can have it.
- He's better than you at swimming – go and get in his way so he comes in last.
- Don't bother to clear up – you want to go on playing.
- Pretend you didn't break that door; then someone else can get the blame.

If we keep doing all these things, whenever we want to please ourselves, we are just like slaves to sin. There are grown-ups who started like this as children and are still like it. But that way doesn't make us happy. We pretend to other people that we like living like this, but really it makes us feel horrid inside and we start not to like ourselves very much. If that's how it is, then we need some help to put things right, so we can be happy and free again.

Over the 'Slaves to sin' sign put up a long piece of paper with the word 'Jesus' written downwards on it, so that you have made a cross, with 'Jesus' crossing out the 'Slaves to sin'. As you do this, explain how Jesus is the one we need to help us, and what he can do is set us free from being slaves to sin! When we decide to follow Jesus, and let his life fill our living, we don't have to live like slaves any more. We are free to work with other people instead of against them all the time. We are free to see that being kind and thoughtful and honest *feels* good because it *is* good. We find that it's more fun to help other people and make them feel better, instead of making them feel sad and frightened.

Now, if we do something selfish, we find we want to put it right quickly and get on with enjoying life again. It's great to be free, instead of being a slave!

Praying

We pray for all people who are slaves to sin,
whether they are children or grown-ups.
We want them all to know you, Jesus,
and we want you to set them free,
so they can live good lives and be happy.

Activities

On the sheet there are instructions for making a slavery chain. The children will need a packet of paper chain strips, or you can make your own from strips of coloured paper and glue. Before they are glued into a chain, the different examples of sin are written on to the links. When the chains are long enough to wear, the children can hang them around their necks, breaking them apart as they pray for Jesus to set free those people who are slaves to sin.

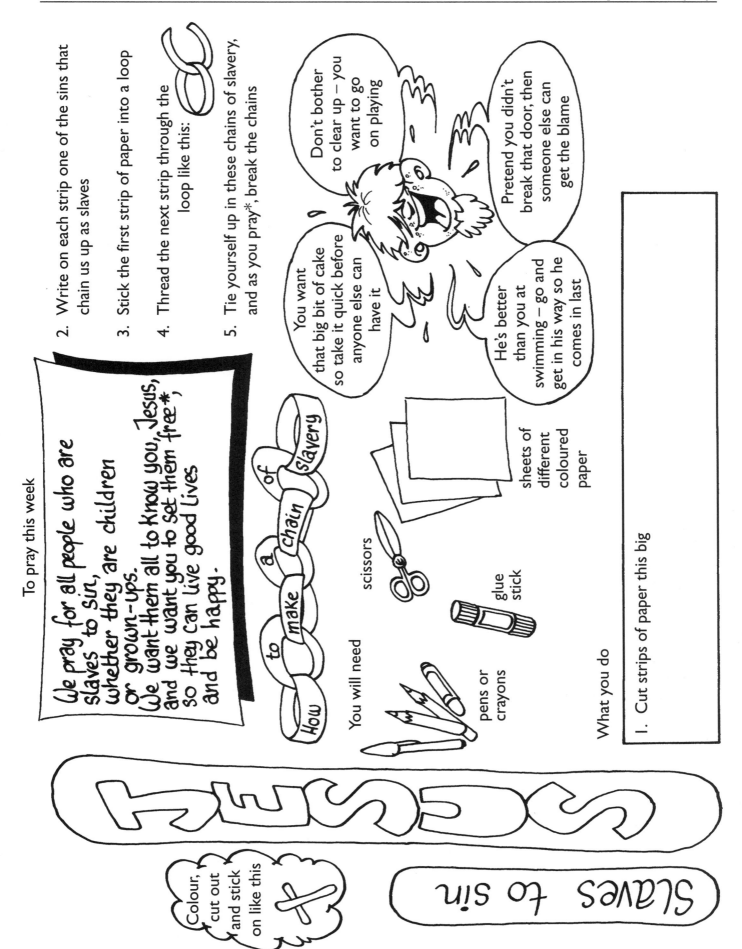

To pray this week

We pray for all people who are slaves to sin, whether they are children or grown-ups. We want them all to know you, Jesus, and we want you to set them free*, so they can live good lives and be happy.

2. Write on each strip one of the sins that chain us up as slaves

3. Stick the first strip of paper into a loop

4. Thread the next strip through the loop like this:

5. Tie yourself up in these chains of slavery, and as you pray*, break the chains

Don't bother to clear up – you want to go on playing

Pretend you didn't break that door, then someone else can get the blame

You want that big bit of cake so take it quick before anyone else can have it

He's better than you at swimming – go and get in his way so he comes in last

How to make a chain of slavery

You will need

scissors

glue stick

pens or crayons

sheets of different coloured paper

What you do

1. Cut strips of paper this big

Colour, cut out and stick on like this

JESUS

Slaves to sin

Proper 9

Sunday between 3 and 9 July inclusive

Thought for the day

To all who are weary with carrying heavy burdens in life, Jesus offers rest for our souls and unthreatening relief.

Readings

Zechariah 9:9-12
Psalm 145:8-14
Romans 7:15-25a
Matthew 11:16-19, 25-30

Aim

To look at how being yoked to Jesus helps us.

Starter

Ask the children to get into pairs and fasten their ankles together with scarves. Everyone can try walking about three-legged, or you could stage a three-legged race.

Teaching

Talk together about what it felt like to be joined up together like that. Draw out the point that it made us all learn to work together with one another very well, because when we worked together we got along really well, without falling down.

Now show the children some pictures from library books of oxen yoked together. Explain how farmers will train a young animal by yoking it up with a good, strong ox who knows what to do. That helps the young ox to learn. Also, the load is not so heavy if two or more animals are sharing it. (You could demonstrate this with two people carrying a handle each of a heavy bag.)

Get a broom handle and lie it along the shoulders of two children. They each hold it in place with both hands. Tell one child to be the leader, and see if they can lead the other child carefully around using the yoke to guide and support.

Now read to the children what Jesus said to all those who are feeling heavily loaded down in life, and they will be able to pick up on the way being yoked to Jesus helps us learn his ways and eases the loads of life.

What are the loads we carry in life? As you talk about some of these, you can pray for people carrying them in a time of intercession.

Praying

Jesus, in you I find rest and peace.
I can talk to you about anything –
my worries and my fears,
my happiness and sadness,
my anger and disappointment.
You always listen and you always understand.

Activities

There is a matching activity on the sheet, working out which loads belong to which bags, and a half-drawn picture to complete symmetrically of oxen ploughing a field. They can also make a load-shaped display of prayer concerns, combining pictures and their own prayers, which can be placed in church to help people pray during the week. Ideas for pictures and prayers are given on the sheet.

Notes

To pray this week

Jesus, in you I find rest and peace.

I can talk to you about anything—
my worries and my fears,
my happiness and sadness,
my anger and disappointment.
You always listen
and you always understand.

Making a prayer concerns board

- Look for pictures in the newspapers
- Draw your own
- Copy a prayer or verse of a hymn
- Write out 'Lord have mercy' to go between the pictures
- Write your own prayers
- Show where in the world the problem is
- Pin up a photograph

WHICH LOAD GOES WHERE?

Half the picture has disappeared! Can you put it back in?

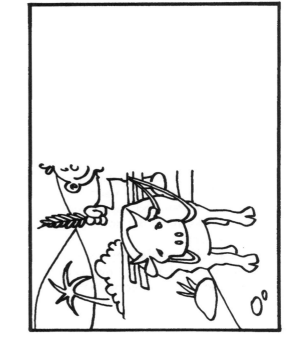

Proper 10

Sunday between 10 and 16 July inclusive

Thought for the day

Seed of God's word, sown in good soil, watered by his rain and warmed by his sunlight, produces a good crop of spiritual fruit.

Readings

Isaiah 55:10-13
Psalm 65:(1-8) 9-13
Romans 8:1-11
Matthew 13:1-9, 18-23

Aim

To know the parable of the sower and the seed, and its meaning.

Starter

If you are able to go outside, see how many different looking leaves or plants you can find in a patch the size of a hula hoop (not the eating sort!). If this is not practical, bring along a number of garden plants that have gone to seed, and harvest the seeds together in various labelled envelopes which can be taken home and planted, or offered to the rest of the congregation after the service.

Teaching

Beforehand prepare a cloth bag like this:

Use some of the seed gathered in the starter activity, or seeds out of a packet, to show the children how you sow seeds in some earth. Then, as long as they have sunlight and water, they will grow. One of the stories Jesus told was about a farmer and what happened to the seed he sowed in his field. As in the all-stage talk (see the *Living Stones* Complete Resource Book), explain how the fields were full of rocky places (put down some sheets of paper to represent these) and there were stony footpaths going across them (put down some footprints).

Place some pearl barley into your cloth bag, and show the children the way farmers in Jesus' country sowed the seed at that time. They walked up and down the field, scattering the seed in handfuls to the left and the right. (They can all try miming this, up and down the room.) It didn't always land on the good, well-prepared soil, though.

In Jesus' story, some of the seed fell on the stony path, where the birds flew down and pecked it up. (They all fly across, cheeping, and pick up the seed on the stony path.)

Some seed fell on the rocky places, where it shot up very fast and then, because it didn't have deep roots, it shrivelled up in the midday sun. (They all crouch down and grow very tall until you show a big yellow sun, at which point they all shrivel up and fall down.)

Some seed fell among thorny weeds at the edges of the field. As it grew, the big tough weeds crowded round it so it never got going. (Name some children as wheat and some as thorny weeds. They all crouch down close together, and the weeds crowd the wheat so that it can't grow properly. No hurting allowed.)

Some seed fell into the good, well-prepared soil that the farmer had ploughed. And here the seed was able to grow up strong and tall, producing a fantastic harvest. (Everyone crouches down and grows up strong and tall, opening out their fingers to be the crop.)

And Jesus didn't tell the people what that story meant. He let them puzzle over it.

Put some quiet music on, and send the children to pick up all the seed that is on the floor, as they puzzle over what the story means.

Praying

Lord Jesus,
some of the things you say
are hard to understand.
But I do know one thing –
God loves us and looks after us
whether we understand everything or not.

Activities

On the sheet the children are helped to understand the meaning of the parable, and also what a parable is.

Notes

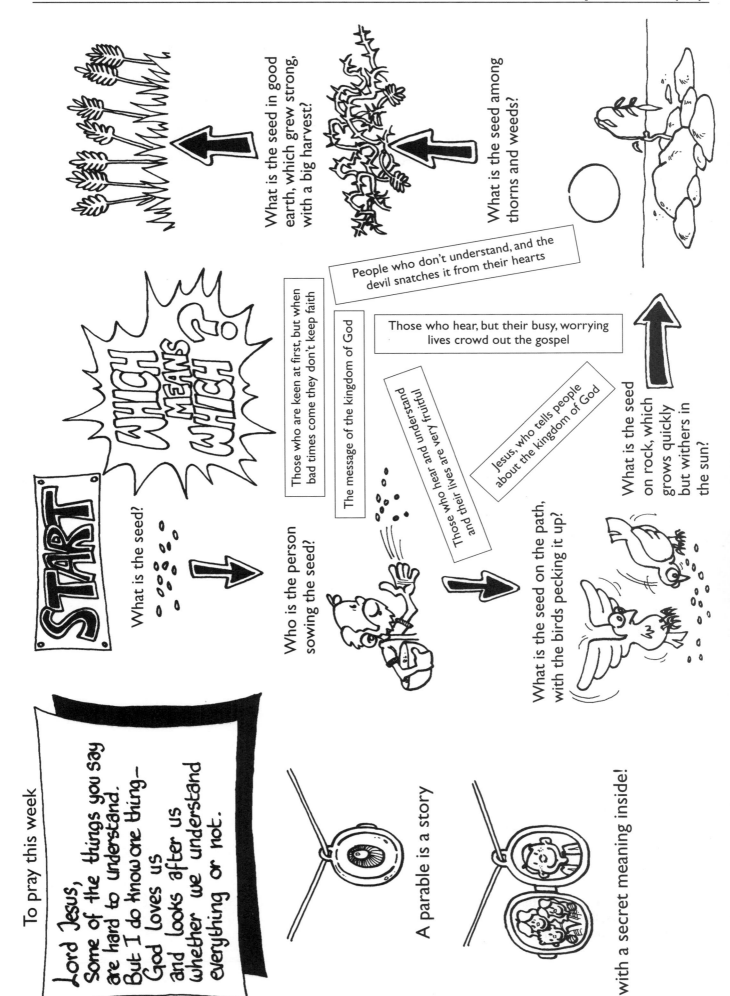

What is the seed in good earth, which grew strong, with a big harvest?

What is the seed among thorns and weeds?

People who don't understand, and the devil snatches it from their hearts

Those who hear, but their busy, worrying lives crowd out the gospel

WHICH WHICH MEANS WHICH?

START

Those who are keen at first, but when bad times come they don't keep faith

The message of the kingdom of God

Those who hear and understand and their lives are very fruitful

Jesus, who tells people about the kingdom of God

What is the seed on rock, which grows quickly but withers in the sun?

What is the seed?

Who is the person sowing the seed?

What is the seed on the path, with the birds pecking it up?

To pray this week

Lord Jesus,
Some of the things you say are hard to understand.
But I do know one thing—
God loves us
and looks after us
whether we understand everything or not.

A parable is a story

with a secret meaning inside!

PROPER 11

Sunday between 17 and 23 July inclusive

Thought for the day

God's justice is always blended with mercy and loving kindness, so that we have real hope.

Readings

Wisdom of Solomon 12:13, 16-19 or Isaiah 44:6-8
Psalm 86:11-17
Romans 8:12-25
Matthew 13:24-30, 36-43

Aim

To know the parable of the wheat and weeds, and its meaning.

Starter

Play a ball (or bean bag) game, first with very unbalanced sides, and then fairly, with equally matched teams.

Teaching

Remind the children of what a parable is, by showing them all one of those sweets which has a surprise in the centre. (Cut it open.) After the story they will get one each, and as they suck on the sweet, they will get to the centre; as they think about Jesus' parable, they'll get to the real meaning of it.

For this story the children will be responding in a particular way whenever certain words are mentioned.

- Farmer – *'Ooh ahh!'*
- Enemy – *'Sssssssssss!'*
- Wheat – Rub tummy and say, *'Yum yum!'*
- Weeds – *'Yuk!'*

Make sure you bring all these words into the story fairly regularly, telling it in your own words or following the suggestion from the all-stage talk in the *Living Stones* Complete Resource Book.

Now give out the sweets as you talk together about what the parable might mean.

Praying

Lord God,
I can see there is evil in this world,
as well as all the good.
Protect us from all evil
and bring us safely to heaven.

Activities

On the sheet there is a pizza to divide very fairly between six children who all like different parts of it. And there is a quiz for them to discover how fair and merciful they are themselves.

Notes

Can you share this pizza fairly?

Rachel doesn't like mushrooms but loves onions

Eleanor doesn't eat meat

Alex likes onions

Barbara, Jessica and Hannah will eat anything!

$\curlyvee$ = mushroom $\frown$ = onion

$\bigcirc$ = pepperoni

COLOUR THIS PIZZA IN.

So now you Know!

3 or more YES
Keep trying – at least you are honest!

3 or more NO
Very fair – just don't get big-headed!

To pray this week

Lord God,
I can see there is evil in this world,
as well as all the good.
Protect us from all evil
and bring us safely to heaven.

HOW FAIR AND JUST ARE YOU?

1. If you were in charge of the picnic would you give yourself the biggest slice of pizza?

No	Perhaps	Yes

2. If you are taking turns at a game, do you take as long as you can?

No	Perhaps	Yes

3. If someone broke your leg during games, would you never forgive them, but hate them for ever?

No	Perhaps	Yes

4. If someone had forgotten their lunch, would you refuse to share yours with them?

No	Perhaps	Yes

PROPER 12

Sunday between 24 and 30 July inclusive

Thought for the day

Jesus, the teacher, enables the ordinary, unlearned people to understand God's wisdom – the eternal laws of his Father's kingdom.

Readings

1 Kings 3:5-12
Psalm 119:129-136
Romans 8:26-39
Matthew 13:31-33, 44-52

Aim

To know that the kingdom of heaven is like a pearl of great value.

Starter

Pearl divers. Scatter some shells or circles of white paper all over the floor. Starting from the edge of the rock (one side of the room), a few children at a time take a deep breath and 'swim' around collecting as many pearls as they can while their breath holds. They must return to the side of the room before taking a new breath.

Teaching

Real pearl divers are often children, who have to swim deep down to collect the shells. There are only pearls in some of the shells, and usually they are quite small, but from time to time you can find a particularly large and beautiful pearl which is worth a great deal of money. They are sold by the pearl sellers to be made into necklaces and brooches. (If you happen to have a pearl necklace, bring it along to show the children.)

Jesus told a story about a pearl seller. In the market all the pearl sellers would have their trays of pearls on show, and everyone would go round looking at them, holding them up to the light, checking for faults, and haggling over the price. (Haggle over the price with either a child or another leader, until you come to an agreement.)

The merchant in Jesus' story was looking around the market for pearls to buy. (Have a child to be the merchant, and others to be selling their pearls. One is holding a velvet covered cushion and on it is a beautiful 'pearl' – a marble, perhaps.) The merchant went from one seller to another, testing the pearls in the light, and checking them carefully for faults. One of the sellers had a velvet cushion, and sitting all on its own in the middle of the cushion was the most magnificent pearl the merchant had ever seen.

(Everyone draws in their breath in amazement at its beauty.)

This pearl had a glow of life about it, and it was large and perfect. The merchant knew that it was far, far more magnificent than anything else he owned, and he wanted to have this beautiful thing. But he didn't have the money to buy it. He thought of everything else he had; nothing seemed as precious to him as this perfect, glowing pearl. So he asked the pearl seller to keep the pearl by for him, and he went off and sold all his other possessions, just so that he had enough money for this one precious pearl. Then he came back with the money and bought it, and was completely happy with what he now had, because it was worth so much more to him than all the other things he had sold.

Praying

Knowing you, Jesus,
is the best thing in my life.
Nothing else is as important
as your love and faithfulness;
nothing else can give me lasting joy and peace.

Activities

On the sheet the children are shown how pearls are made, and there are instructions for making a pearl in a shell prayer. Each child will need a small lump of self-hardening clay, or some salt dough (two cups of flour, one cup of salt, water to mix).

Notes

How to make a pearl in a shell

You will need

a template

water

clay

a knife

How to make it

1. Cut out this template

2. Roll a clay ball the size of a marble

3. Roll out the rest of the clay

4. Put the template on it and cut out a shell shape. Do this again so you have two

5. Wet your hands. Join the two shell shapes at the narrow ends

6. Put this week's prayer inside

7. Put the clay ball on top of the prayer

8. You have made a pearl in a shell. When it is dry you can paint it if you like

HOW PEARLS ARE MADE...

1. The shell is in the sea

OUCH!

2. A bit of grit gets in the shell

THAT FEELS BETTER!

3. The bit of grit is covered with mother-of-pearl to make it smooth

To pray this week

Knowing you, Jesus, is the best thing in my life. Nothing else is as important as your love and faithfulness; nothing else can give me lasting joy and peace.

PROPER 13

Thought for the day

God feeds all who come to him hungry, and we, as the Church, are expected to share in that work.

Readings

Isaiah 55:1-5
Psalm 145:8-9, 14-21
Romans 9:1-5
Matthew 14:13-21

Aim

To know that Jesus knows our needs and provides for us.

Starter

What do I need? One of the children is given an identity or work label, such as postman or ice-cream seller. The others have to work out the identity by asking them what they would need to do this job of work.

Teaching

Have a number of cards with these words on, illustrated simply, to help with reading: food, air, rest, sleep, hobbies, friendship, water, shelter, fashionable clothes, love, air, TV, chocolate, exercise, God. Have two heading cards: 'Wants' and 'Needs'.

Working together, decide which of these are wants and which are needs. This will mean looking at the things we actually need to survive and the things we think we need but which are only really extras, however nice they are. Sometimes people don't realise what they really need.

Really they need sleep but because they don't want to waste their time sleeping, they have a strong cup of coffee to keep them awake. That's OK sometimes, but if we start to live like it all the time it's bad for us. Really they need to feel loved, but instead of going to God and getting the love they need, they eat loads of sweets to comfort themselves, or drink loads of beer. And if they do this all the time it's bad for them.

(Place a piggy bank on the floor.) Sometimes we get let down or cheated by things we bought because we thought we wanted them and then found they didn't make us as happy as we hoped they would. Sometimes people think that being rich will make them happy, but real, lasting happiness doesn't come from being rich or having lots of things. Real happiness comes from God's love, which you don't even need to save up for, because

he gives it to us free. However rich you are and however poor you are, God's love is free and will give you what you really need as a human being. It doesn't cheat you or let you down; it feeds you, just as a good meal feeds your body.

Praying

The Lord is my shepherd,
there is nothing else I need.
He leads me and he feeds me
all the days of my life.
O Lord, my shepherd,
you are all I need.

Activities

On the sheet there is the story of the feeding of the five thousand, told with pictures and code words. There is also a chart to show how God's love can be spread if we start it off, so that many are fed in a way that satisfies. They can also wrap up sweets with messages on and give them away freely just as they were given God's love freely.

Notes

HOW GOD'S LOVE SPREADS

➡ = is loving to

To pray this week

The Lord is my Shepherd,
there is nothing else I need.
He leads me and he feeds me
all the days of my life.
O Lord, my Shepherd,
you are all I need.

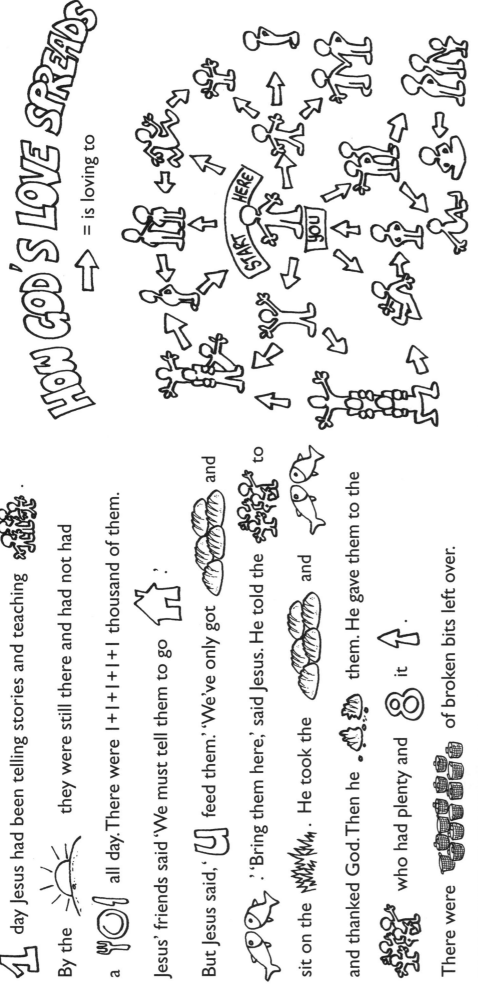

1 day Jesus had been telling stories and teaching [figure].

By the [sun] they were still there and had not had

a [plate] all day. There were 1+1+1+1+1 thousand of them.

Jesus' friends said 'We must tell them to go [house].

But Jesus said, '[hand] feed them.' 'We've only got [bread] and

[fish] ': 'Bring them here,' said Jesus. He told the [people] to

sit on the [grass]. He took the [bread] and

and thanked God. Then he [broke] them. He gave them to the

[people] who had plenty and 8 it [house].

There were [baskets] of broken bits left over.

PROPER 14

Thought for the day

God is faithful to us through all the storms of life, yet our faith in God is so very small.

Readings

1 Kings 19:9-18
Psalm 85:8-13
Romans 10:5-15
Matthew 14:22-33

Aim

To know the story of Jesus on the water, and Peter walking to him.

Starter

If the weather is fine, have a paddling pool outside and some toy boats, or floating tubs to play with. Otherwise, have a number of washing-up bowls on plastic sheeting indoors.

Teaching

One way of telling today's story is with a parachute. Everyone stands around the edge and the parachute becomes the sea, which can be made very still and calm, and various other stages of roughness to a roaring storm. Practise this with the children first, giving a clear signal for following the leader's instructions, so that they get good at all responding together. As you tell the story, use the parachute sea and its natural sound effects, with everyone shouting above the storm: 'Help! It's a ghost!'

Or you can get everyone making the sound effects of the storm and waves with percussion instruments, rubbing their palms together, tapping fingers on palms and using voices. For this have most people sitting in the form of a boat, and rocking in unison as the waves get worse, and a few, including Peter, inside the 'boat'. Then Peter can climb out of the boat towards Jesus.

Praying

Be with me, Lord Jesus,
through the storms in my life,
through the times
when I'm frightened or angry or sad.
Teach me to trust you with all of myself
through the good times and through the bad.

Activities

On the sheet there are instructions for making a working model of a stormy sea. The children will need thin card to strengthen the model.

Notes

94

How to make a stormy sea

1. Colour all the sea blue and green
2. Colour the boat, cut out, fold and stick
3. Cut slits on A
4. Fold B like this
5. Stick card strip inside middle like this and cut top to look like this

6. Push the stormy waves up and down through the slits

To pray this week

Be with me, Lord Jesus, through the storms in my life, through the times when I'm frightened or angry or sad. Teach me to trust you with all of myself through the good times and through the bad.

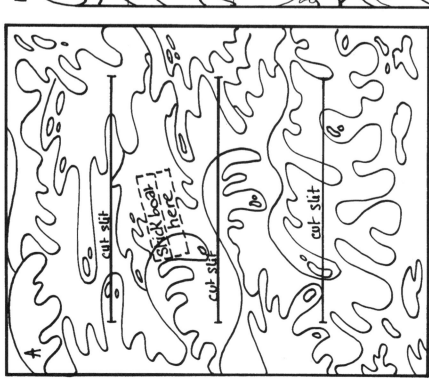

cut slit

Stick boat here

cut slit

cut slit

fold

Cut strip of card this size!

PROPER 15

Sunday between 14 and 20 August inclusive

Thought for the day

The good news of salvation is not limited to a particular group or nation but available for the whole world.

Readings

Isaiah 56:1, 6-8
Psalm 67
Romans 11:1-2a, 29-32
Matthew 15:(10-20) 21-28

Aim

To know that the Gospel is for all nations.

Starter

Tell the children a selection of different greetings, and set them off walking around to music. Whenever the music stops, call out a nationality, and everyone goes round greeting one another appropriately. Here are some suggestions for greetings:

British – shake hands and say, 'How do you do?' 'How do you do?'

Japanese – hands together and bow to each other

American Indian – raise hand and say 'How!' or rub noses

Australian – 'G'day!'

French – kiss both cheeks or say, 'Bonjour!'

Teaching

Bring along a world map and a selection of books on different life patterns in various countries, with tasters of various foods from around the world. (Many supermarkets have quite a wide selection of breads; other items might be dates, bananas, yams, rice and raw cane sugar.)

You could either introduce these in the circle or have it set up more as a 'market place' with the children walking round looking and sampling while music from other cultures is playing. Then come back and see where some of these places are on the world map. If the map is placed on a table they can be marked with nightlight candles.

Remind the children of how the whole world is God's, and he made it. Use the cut-out sections of the diagram below to explain how God made a promise to Abraham long before Jesus was born: that he would make his family into a chosen nation, and that through this nation the whole world would be blessed. When Jesus came, the second part of that promise started to come true, and it's still

coming true now, as more and more of the world hears the good news of God's love.

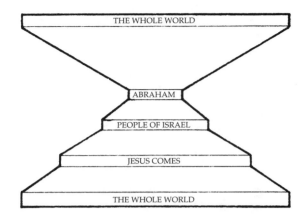

It hasn't been completed yet though. That's why we all pray in the Lord's prayer, 'Let your kingdom come'. There are still people in our world who do not know and need telling. It may well be that some of the children here will spread the Gospel, so that eventually everyone will know.

Praying

God, bless our world.
Help us to look after it
and to look after one another.
Let your kingdom come in our world
and let your will be done,
so it is filled with peace and love. Amen.

Activities

Through coded puzzles on the sheet the children are taken through from the promise to Abraham up to the hope for all the world. They are also encouraged to pray for the world Church and make links with a group of Christians in another part of the world.

Notes

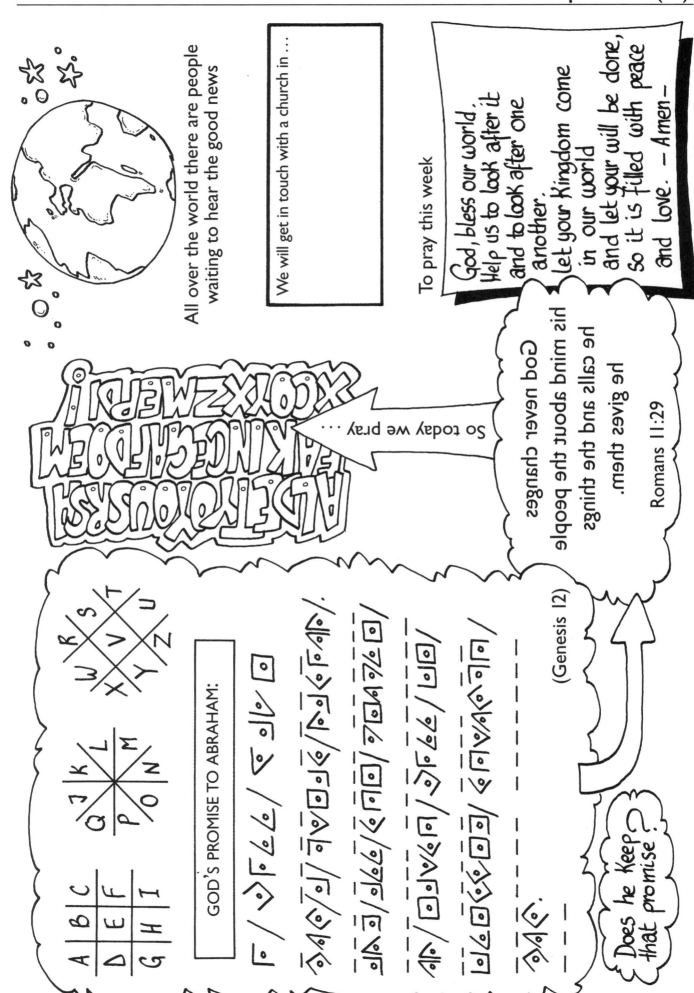

PROPER 16

Sunday between 21 and 27 August inclusive

Thought for the day

The Church is the Body of Christ, built on strong rock of faith and energised by the living Breath of God.

Readings

Isaiah 51:1-6
Psalm 138
Romans 12:1-8
Matthew 16:13-20

Aim

To know about Peter's confession of faith.

Starter

Who am I? Stick a picture of an animal or person on someone's back. This person turns round so the other children can see the picture. The volunteer asks questions to determine his/her identity, to which all the other children can only say 'yes' or 'no'.

Teaching

Give clues about a particular child in the group until the identity is guessed correctly – for example, this person likes Irish dancing . . . wears glasses . . . has a wobbly tooth . . . and is seven. It must be Rory! Today we are going to hear about someone else. See if you can work out who it is.

Imagine you live in a village. Not far from your house is a sea, and your dad is a fisherman. You often walk down to the beach and help him sort out the fishing nets, and mend any rips in them. Over the past year or so life has changed in your village because of a man who walks around the country with a group of friends. Everyone in your village knows about him. One person used to be so deaf she couldn't hear a thing, but she went to this man and now she can hear as well as you. Your next door neighbour couldn't walk very well, but he can now because this man made the leg better.

Every so often someone will come running into your village shouting that this man is talking by the lake, and suddenly everyone comes out of their houses, or stops what they're doing, and you all set off for the beach, just because this man is going to be there. And when you get there, you find crowds of other people from other villages have come as well, settling themselves down on the beach and the grass, looking towards a man who is sitting in one of the fishing boats. He doesn't look anything special. He's just wearing ordinary clothes, and he isn't shouting or waving his arms around or anything.

But everyone feels good when he's there. He has this strange way of making you feel important and special and yet able to be really yourself. People are kind to each other, making room for one another and helping the old ones sit down. This man seems to make you all want to behave well, just because he is so lovely himself. He tells stories, and gets you thinking about what life is really all about, and then he starts walking quietly around, praying with people, laying his hands on them and making them better, listening to them and comforting them. Some people have brought food, and often it all turns into a picnic, with the man enjoying the food he's been given, talking and smiling with you, interested in you.

When he has to move on to another area, you all wave and walk with him away from the beach, before going back to work as usual in the village. But the day seems happier and brighter because the man has been to visit you. Who is this man – is it John the Baptist? Is it Elijah or one of the prophets? The man is . . . Jesus, the Christ, the Son of God.

Praying

Lord Jesus, I can see
that you must really be
the Son of God our Father,
because you speak God's word
and live God's love,
and there is no one else like you.

Activities

The sheet helps them to look at Simon Peter's confession of faith and the things that made him realise who Jesus was. There is also a code sum to change Simon into Peter and discover the meaning of his new name.

> ## Notes

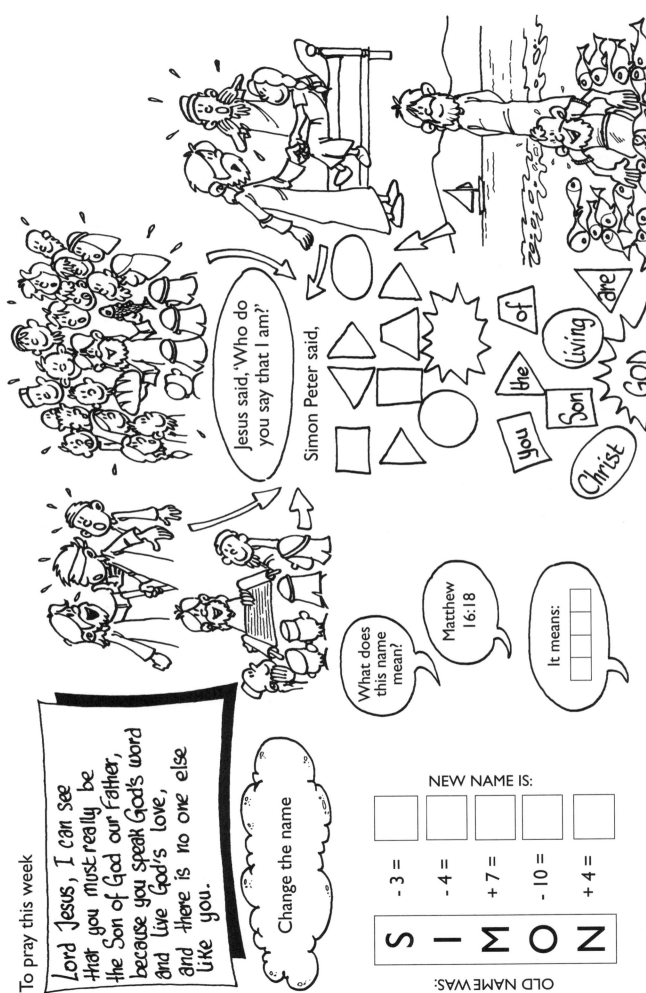

Jesus said, 'Who do you say that I am?'

Simon Peter said,

What does this name mean?

Matthew 16:18

It means:

To pray this week

Lord Jesus, I can see that you must really be the Son of God our Father, because you speak God's word and live God's love, and there is no one else like you.

Change the name

NEW NAME IS:

OLD NAME WAS:

S I M O N

- 3 =
- 4 =
+ 7 =
- 10 =
+ 4 =

A B C D E F G H I J K L M N O P Q R S T U V W X Y Z

PROPER 17

Thought for the day

As Jesus prepares for the necessary suffering of the cross, he is tempted, through well-meaning friendship, to avoid it.

Readings

Jeremiah 15:15-21
Psalm 26:1-8
Romans 12:9-21
Matthew 16:21-28

Aim

To look at why Jesus set his face to Jerusalem.

Starter

All change! Set the children walking or hopping or jumping, and every time you clap your hands they change direction, and the method of movement also changes.

Teaching

Draw the following outlines on thin card to be road junctions, and have a toy car to drive along them.

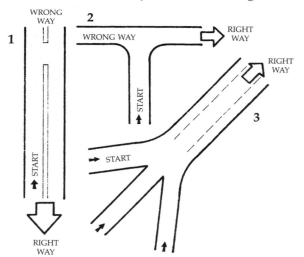

If you are driving along in the wrong direction, you can make a U-turn to go right round and go back the way you came (1). Sometimes you come to a junction, where you have to choose whether to go to the right or the left (2). And sometimes the road you are driving on turns into a new, important road, with more lanes to it, and all you do is carry on in the same direction for this next stage of the road. (3)

These things happen to us in life as well. If we are living wrongly, it's like driving in the wrong direction, and we have to make a U-turn to get right again (1). Often in life we are at those junctions, where we have to choose whether to go one way or another, whether to do what is right or please ourselves and do what is wrong (2). (And if we make the wrong choice, we'll be back at that U-turn!)

Jesus seemed to be at one of those junctions (2) just after Peter had recognised him as the Christ, the Son of the living God. He knew that he had been sent to earth to save us all, and he knew that would be expensive. Not in money, but in life. Jesus knew that the only way he could set us free was to suffer and die for us. So here was the junction – was he willing to go through all that for us . . . or not? The Gospel of Matthew tells us that he was willing, and he started getting his disciples ready for the terrible things that would happen to him at Jerusalem.

In fact, his road had just turned into a new stretch of road (3) – all Jesus was doing was carrying on with the same loving direction he had always had. But now Peter was at a junction (2). He didn't like to hear Jesus talking about having to suffer and die – he didn't want his good friend to suffer at all! Yet if Jesus was saying it, then it must be all part of God's good plan. Peter couldn't cope with that at the moment, so he chose the other way and said to Jesus, 'Never, Lord! This shall never happen to you!'

So now Jesus was at a junction (2). What do you think would have happened if he had agreed with Peter, instead of going on with God's plan? We could never have been set free! So it was a rather important choice for Jesus to make. He chose the loving way – to go through with the saving plan, even though he knew it would be terribly painful and cost him everything. That's how much he loved us. And what about Peter, still driving along the wrong way (1)? Jesus helped him to make a good U-turn so he was back in the right direction again.

Praying

Jesus, it must have been very hard to go to Jerusalem, knowing you would be going to lose your life there. Thank you for loving us enough to do it.

Activities

On the sheet there are the different road shapes so that if you provide microcars (or buttons) they can decide which road is which for the suggested situations in life. There is the possibility for discussion here about friends leading and being led in wrong directions, and leaders need to be aware that some children may need practical help in standing up for what they know is right in difficult circumstances.

Proper 18

Sunday between 4 and 10 September inclusive

Thought for the day

It is our responsibility to encourage and uphold one another in living by the standard of real love.

Readings

Ezekiel 33:7-11
Psalm 119:33-40
Romans 13:8-14
Matthew 18:15-20

Aim

To know we are to help one another live in God's way.

Starter

Give everyone a building brick (all different sizes and colours) and a drawn plan of the tower they are all going to build. They help one another to get the bricks in the right places, so the tower is completed. They can each only handle their own brick.

Teaching

Have an outlined person cut from thin card or paper, which is split into chunks as shown below.

Point out to the children how they all helped one another in the tower building, and if someone noticed that a brick was in the wrong place they helped to change it. We all belong to the Church of God, and we have to work together, helping one another so that the church can be what it is meant to be – the Body of Christ (fix the body together so everyone can read it).

(Put down a pair of binoculars.) If I want to look at the moon, and see it clearly, I can use these binoculars to help me. Suppose I was looking at a group of Christians. The binoculars I'd be looking through would be magic ones, so that I could see not just what they looked like but what they were

really like as people, and how they behaved. (Look through your binoculars at the group.) What do you think I would see?

Collect all their ideas, which may include such things as looking just like everyone else, going to church, praying, reading the Bible, loving God, helping people, loving people, trying to be good and making mistakes but wanting to put them right. It's true that people with magic binoculars should be able to look at Christians and see that we are loving, honest, kind and friendly, but most of all they should be able to see that we know we are loved and forgiven by the God who made us. They should be able to see that we know and love the true God.

How can we help one another to be like this? (Get the bricks and build them up as the ideas are mentioned.)

- We can pray together and for one another.
- We can cheer one another out of bad moods.
- We can say if we think something is wrong.
- We can be keen and join in at church so others can see we mean it.
- We can listen and look so we notice if someone is sad or worried.
- We can be a good example by how we behave.

That way we will be working in God's team, as he has called us to do, helping and encouraging one another so that as a church, as the Body of Christ, we can all be used to make the world a better and happier place.

Praying

Here I am, Lord.
Help me to live your way
and help me to work with others
so that we can be part of your team.

Activities

On the sheet the children can work out which qualities are the ones we want to build up in one another, and which we want to have sorted out. They can also put into practice the prayer-partner idea, using the form provided.

Notes

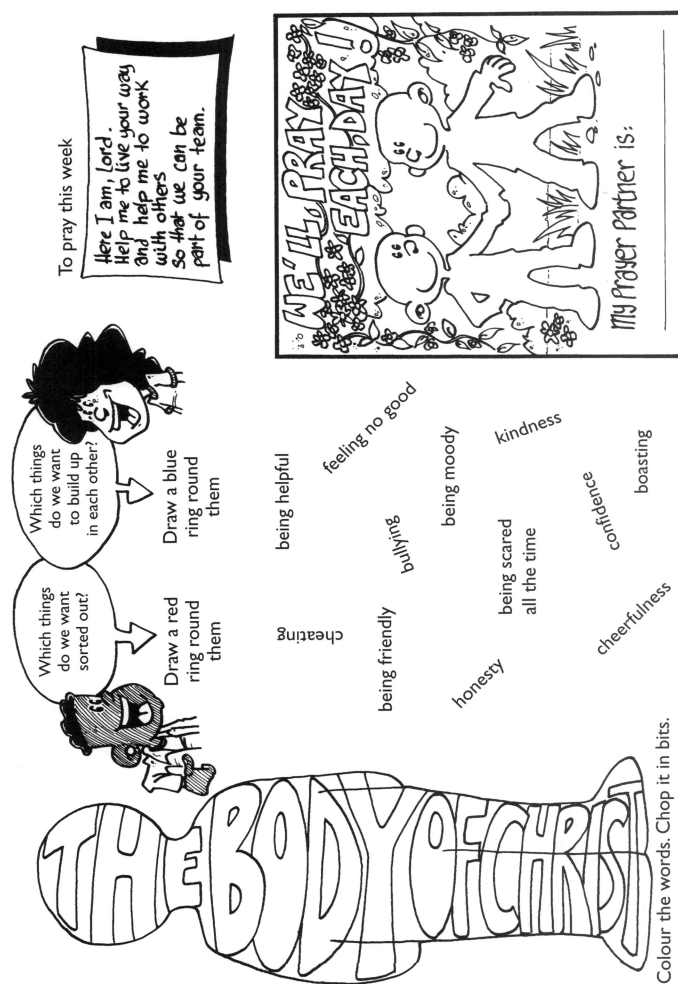

To pray this week

Here I am, Lord.
Help me to live your way
and help me to work
with others
so that we can be
part of your team.

WE'LL PRAY EACH DAY!

My Prayer Partner is: _____

Which things do we want to build up in each other?

Draw a blue ring round them

Which things do we want sorted out?

Draw a red ring round them

being helpful

feeling no good

kindness

bullying

being moody

boasting

confidence

cheating

being scared all the time

being friendly

cheerfulness

honesty

THE BODY OF CHRIST

Colour the words. Chop it in bits.
Put it all together again.

Proper 19

Sunday between 11 and 17 September inclusive

Thought for the day

Forgiving is a natural result of loving, so it is not an option for us but a command.

Readings

Genesis 50:15-21
Psalm 103:(1-7) 8-13
Romans 14:1-12
Matthew 18:21-35

Aim

To know the parable of the unforgiving servant and explore its meaning.

Starter

Help everyone to feel their heartbeat or pulse. Explain that we are going to do an experiment and find out what happens to our heartbeat when we do exercise. Then lead them in running on the spot, star jumps and frog hops for a while, or dance to some praise music. Now everyone feels their pulse again. Is it any different? What have we discovered? That when we move about fast, our heart beats faster.

Teaching

The natural result of moving about is that our heart beats faster. What is the natural result of sitting in the sun? We get hot. What's the natural result of putting the plug in a washbasin and turning on the taps? We get a basin filled with water. What's the natural result of climbing into a swimming pool? We get wet. Lots of things happen naturally as a result of something else.

Wanting to forgive is the natural result of loving. It's what happens. God forgives us because he loves us so much. We're not always so keen to forgive when people have done things to upset us, and Jesus told one of his parables (his stories with secret meanings) about it to help us.

You will need three puppets, made from socks or paper bags as shown.

Give the script in the Appendix, page 134, to three children to read, and sit them down behind a table placed on its side, so the puppets show over the top.

Praying

Father, if you are so kind
and forgiving to us,
we need to be kind and forgiving
to one another.
Please help us.

Activities

On the sheet there are a couple of maths machines to work out, and a puzzle to help them explore why we find it hard to forgive, and how we can learn to do it better.

Notes

Proper 20

Thought for the day

We have no right to be envious at the generosity and mercy God shows to others.

Readings

Jonah 3:10-4:11
Psalm 145:1-8
Philippians 1:21-30
Matthew 20:1-16

Aim

To know the parable of the workmen in the vineyard and explore its meaning.

Starter

Vineyard. Go through the following actions with the children first: vine-planting, watering, weeding, grape-picking, grape-treading, and bottling, appointing a particular area of the room for each task. Call out the tasks and everyone runs to the place and mimes it. Make the change-arounds from task to task quite speedy, and use each task any number of times and in any order. The last person to start doing the job each time is 'fired' until the winner is left.

Teaching

Today's parable is all about some people who worked in a vineyard. As they already know, there's a lot of work to do in vineyards! Tell the story as it is in Matthew 20, involving the children to act it out as you tell it. The ones who are employed can do the actions from the starter activity, with the odd break session included. Make it quite clear that the workers and the boss were happy to agree on the day's wage before they started work.

Did the workers get what they had agreed was fair for a day's work? Yes, they did. Jesus was showing the people that God will always treat us fairly, giving us what we need, but if he wants to be generous we shouldn't get grumpy about it. The vineyard owner wanted to see everyone who needed a job being able to work, so he was happy to pay them all a fair day's wage, rather than just the first ones.

Praying

Lord, help me to be generous like you,
wanting the best for everyone,
and not just for me and my friends.

Activities

On the sheet the children find out about another grumpy person – Jonah under his olive plant. They can make the model with a plant that grows.

Notes

Cut piece of green plastic bag like this for the castor oil plant

CUT ALONG HERE

Cut slit **B**

Cut slit here

Cut slit **A**

Stick bottom of plant here

Fold back

1. Colour the picture
2. Make the plant
3. Fold back the flap and stick plant inside
4. Poke end of plant out of slit **A**, so it can grow when you pull
5. Fix plant in slit **B** to shade Grumpy Jonah
6. Pull plant back down to wither it

GRUMPY JONAH

Jonah was grumpy. He was cross because Nineveh had turned back to God and was safe. (Jonah hated Nineveh.) He sat and sulked.

God made a castor oil plant grow up over his head to shade him. Jonah liked it. Then the plant withered away. Jonah was angry and sad. God said, 'You are bothered about one plant! Can't you see now, how bothered I was by a big city like Nineveh? I wanted to have those people safe, and I'm glad they are.'

To pray this week

Lord, help me to be generous like you, wanting the best for everyone, and not just for me and my friends.

PROPER 21

Sunday between 25 September and 1 October inclusive

Thought for the day

God longs for us to die to sin and live, but it has to be our choice, too.

Readings

Ezekiel 18:1-4, 25-32
Psalm 25:1-9
Philippians 2:1-13
Matthew 21:23-32

Aim

To know we have to choose whether to work with God or against him.

Starter

Beforehand prepare a number of pieces of drinking straw holding rolled-up numbers. Half these numbers (all of which are in the same colour straw) end with a 0. The children choose a straw and see if it has a 0 in the number. If it has they can have a sweet or a sticker. Draw their attention to the colour of the winning straws. Have enough winning ones for everyone to have one if they choose the right colour.

Teaching

Talk about the choices we make all day long – what to have for breakfast, whether to brush our teeth or pretend we have already brushed them, whether to play football or chat with friends, whether to share our crisps or eat them all ourselves, whether to work hard or waste our time. Some of these choices don't matter much, but when they are choosing between good or bad, kind or unkind, then they matter very much.

One of the parables Jesus told was about two brothers. Their dad was yet another vineyard owner – there are a lot of vineyards in Israel (you could have a bottle of wine from that area to prove it) so that is why Jesus used them a lot in his stories. Today he would probably talk about owners of video shops or supermarkets. Anyway, the dad went to one of his sons and said, 'Off you go and work in the vineyard, son.' And his son turned round and said to his dad, 'No, I'm not going to.' But later on he changed his mind, and went.

Then the dad went to his other son, and said the same thing to him: 'Off you go and work in the vineyard, son.' This son jumped up and said to his dad (very politely), 'Yes, sir, I will!' But he didn't actually go.

Which of these two brothers did what his father wanted? When the children have told you, find the place in Matthew 21 and show them how they have just answered the question Jesus asked the people listening to his story. And it's the right answer. What is Jesus telling us all in this parable? Who is the father? It's God. Who are the brothers? All of us. When are we like the first brother? When are we like the second brother? What is most important to God – hearing us say we will follow him and do his work in our life, or watching us choosing to do something about it?

Praying

Lord, teach me to choose good, not bad,
to choose kindness, not cruelty,
to choose honesty, not lies,
to choose right, not wrong. Amen.

Activities

There are instructions on the sheet for making a paperweight which they can use to think about their actions and whether they are working with God or against him. Suggest they use it as follows: at the start of each day choose to live God's way. At the end of each day think over what has happened. As you think of the selfish things, turn the paperweight to the 'My way' side. Tell God you are sorry. As you think of the good things, turn it to the 'God's way' side again. Each child will need a small lump of self-hardening clay or some salt dough (two cups of flour, one cup of salt, water to mix). It is also made quite clear that God knows they are not to blame for someone else's wrong, and they need never feel to blame for something bad which someone might have done to them. Be sensitive, here, to any children who are living with this kind of guilt.

Notes

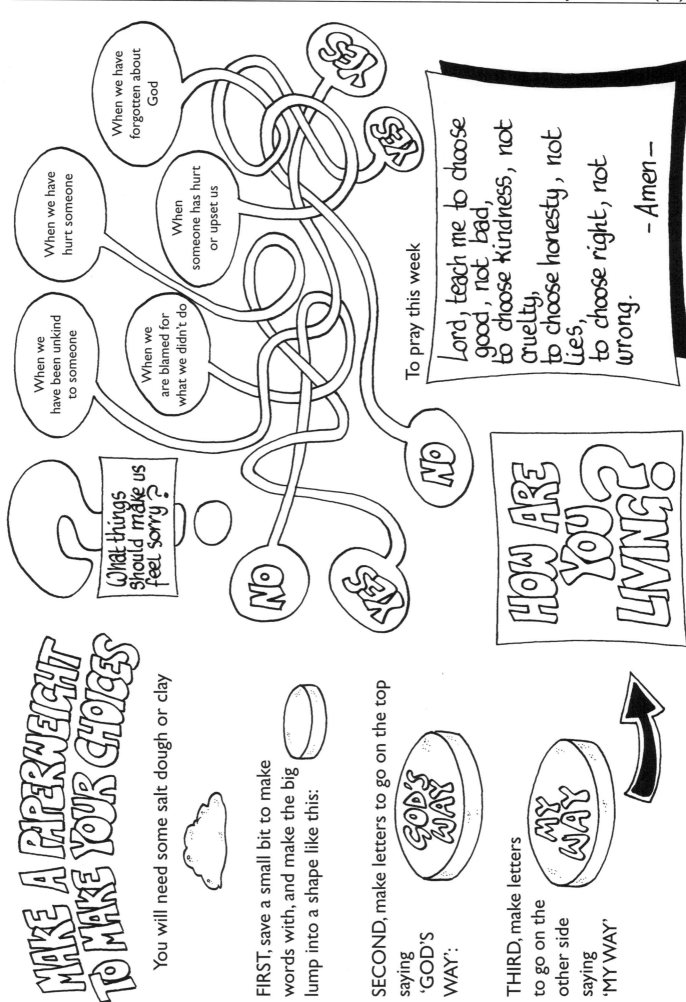

PROPER 22

Sunday between 2 and 8 October inclusive

Thought for the day

God does everything possible for our spiritual growth and well-being, but still we can choose hostility and rejection.

Readings

Isaiah 5:1-7
Psalm 80:7-15
Philippians 3:4b-14
Matthew 21:33-46

Aim

To know the two parables of the vineyard and their meanings.

Starter

Come and sit on my friend's chair! One person goes out of the room, and the others arrange themselves in a row, each standing behind a chair. They agree on which chair is going to be the 'right' one to sit on. When the person comes in, everyone tries to encourage them to sit on their friend's chair and the person chooses one and sits down. If it's the 'right' one, they get a cheer and applause; if it isn't, they get tipped off and a thumbs-down. Then it's someone else's turn to go outside.

Teaching

Today we are looking at some people who found it very hard to recognise the truth when they saw it, and we'll be looking at what it feels like to be chucked out and rejected.

To help tell this week's parables, prepare some cut paper shapes of appropriate colours, as shown below.

Set A

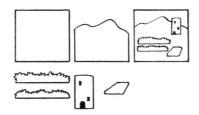

Set B

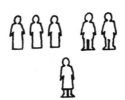

As you tell the parable from Isaiah, place the shapes from set A, one by one, on to a sheet of plain paper. In the Isaiah story the pieces will then be gradually taken away again until there is nothing left. Help the children to work out who's who in this story, and what it might mean. Then put down the words of verse 7 and everyone can read them together:

The vineyard belonging to the Lord is the nation of Israel,
his carefully planted garden is the people of Judah;
the Lord looked for justice but all he found was killing;
the Lord hoped for right living but there were only cries of pain.

Explain that many generations later, Jesus was trying to get the religious leaders to recognise who he was, but he was having a hard time getting through to them because they didn't want to hear. (Like us when someone calls out that it's bedtime and we accidentally on purpose don't hear them and carry on playing!) Jesus chose a story they would already know, as the children will see, but at one point it changes. See if they can spot where this is. As they listen to the story, they can pretend they are the religious leaders, who don't approve of Jesus, and have just challenged him to tell them who on earth he thinks he is.

Use the shapes again, building up the picture just as before, but go on to the shapes in set B. See if anyone has spotted the point of change, and then draw out what they think this parable means, and what the leaders would think as they listened to it. (The vineyard and planted vine are still the same, the servants are God's prophets, sent to speak out God's words, and the son is Jesus, God's Son. Being thrown out and killed is being rejected and crucified.)

Praying

Keep our ears open, Lord,
to hear what you want us to hear.

Activities

The sheet can be made into a stand-up model of a vineyard so that the children can build it up as they go over the parable.

Notes

110

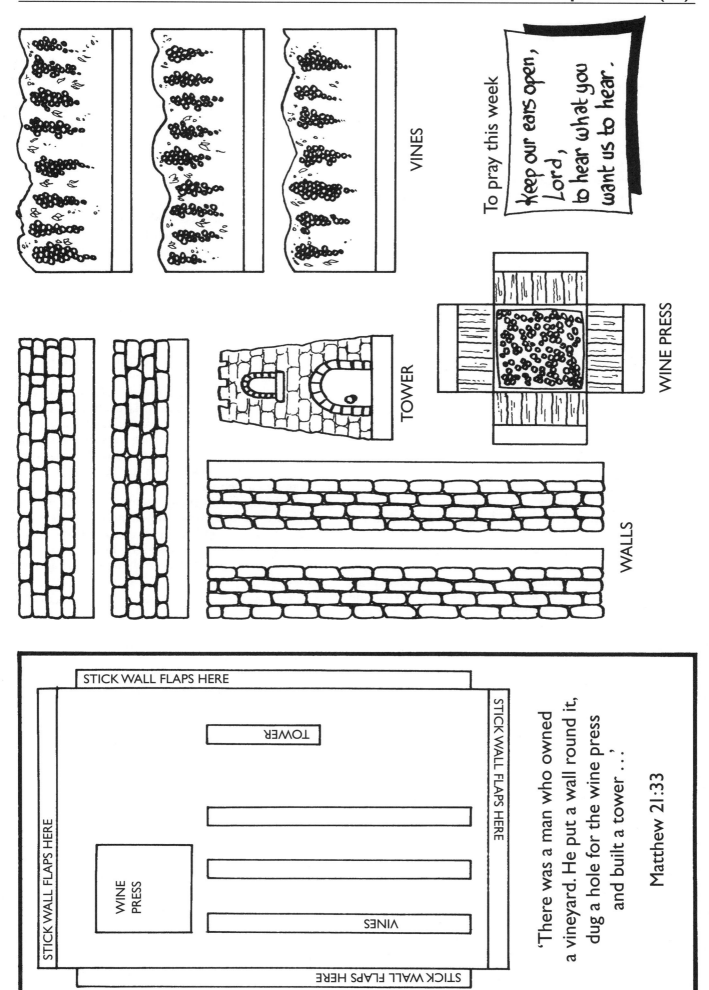

VINES

To pray this week

Keep our ears open, Lord, to hear what you want us to hear.

WINE PRESS

TOWER

WALLS

STICK WALL FLAPS HERE

STICK WALL FLAPS HERE

STICK WALL FLAPS HERE

STICK WALL FLAPS HERE

TOWER

WINE PRESS

VINES

'There was a man who owned a vineyard. He put a wall round it, dug a hole for the wine press and built a tower . . .'

Matthew 21:33

PROPER 23

Sunday between 9 and 15 October inclusive

Thought for the day

We are all invited to God's wedding banquet; in accepting we must allow the rags of our old life to be exchanged for the freely given robes of holiness and right living.

Readings

Isaiah 25:1-9
Psalm 23
Philippians 4:1-9
Matthew 22:1-14

Aim

To know the parable of the wedding feast and begin to look at its meaning.

Starter

Can I come to the party? Everyone sits along the wall at one end of the room, taking turns to throw a dice. When someone throws a six, everyone stands up and calls out to the leader at the other end, 'Can I come to the party?' The leader calls back, 'Only if you're wearing blue and white/had no breakfast/have a sister . . .' Then those allowed to come to the party go into the middle for a short, loud snatch of music and dancing, before returning to the wall and continuing to throw dice.

Teaching

Bring along enough pieces of fabric, towels, sheets and scarves for everyone to be given one. They are all helped to dress in these and then sit down to listen to the story.

Tell the children about the way kings used to have wardrobes full of special clothes for visitors, so that whenever people were invited to a party at the palace, they would be given one of the king's robes to wear just as we have all been fitted out with a robe today. That was all part of the invitation.

Jesus told a parable about a king who threw a party. It was a wedding party for his son, and all the guests were invited. But they all refused to come; they didn't want to celebrate the prince's wedding, and they made feeble excuses, and went off to make money instead. The king was very

angry and punished them all. But he still needed guests for the party. So he sent his servants out to stand at all the crossroads and invite the ordinary people passing by to come to the grand celebration as guests of the king.

In they all came, crowds of them. Some were good people, some were bad; the king didn't mind – he wanted to invite everyone, with no one left out. As everyone came in with their old, scruffy clothes on, the servants in charge of the king's wardrobe sorted out a wedding garment for them all, and shooed them into the great hall which was all decorated, loaded with food and drink, and well lit with candles at all the tables.

The ordinary people were thrilled – they'd never thought they would ever be invited to a party at the king's palace, and they really enjoyed themselves. The king came in and looked around, glad to have the great hall filled with happy guests, celebrating his son's wedding. As he walked around, he suddenly had a shock. One of the guests was insulting the king who had invited him to this honour. He was not wearing the special robe he had been given, but was sitting there in dirty rags. The king went up to him. 'Friend,' he said, surprised, 'how come you aren't wearing a wedding garment at this important wedding party?' The man was speechless, and the king had him thrown outside. How dare he expect to be part of the celebration if he couldn't even be bothered to change.

So inside the great hall, all the invited guests had the time of their lives. They danced and sang and ate and drank and laughed. And outside, in the cold darkness, stood those who had refused to be part of the celebration, even though they had been invited.

Praying

Father God, you have invited us,
just as we are, to your kingdom.
You forgive us our sins
and clothe us in your robes of goodness.
You satisfy our hunger and our thirst,
and make us happy.
Thank you, Father God,
for all your goodness to us.

Activities

On the sheet the children are led to work out what the secret meaning of this parable is, both for the people listening to Jesus at the time, and for us today. They can use the pictures to show the story on a matchbox television (instructions included), and also enjoy a festive time of praise and dancing, with streamer and flag waving, and some taped praise songs to sing along with.

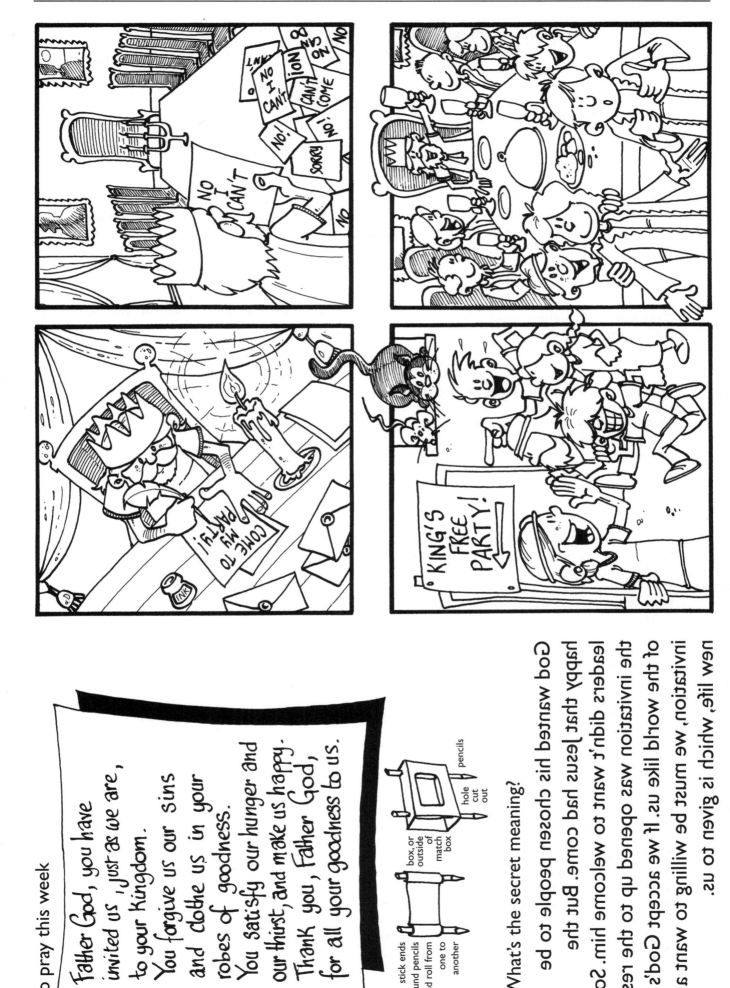

To pray this week

Father God, you have
invited us, just as we are,
to your Kingdom.
You forgive us our sins
and clothe us in your
robes of goodness.
You satisfy our hunger and
our thirst, and make us happy.
Thank you, Father God,
for all your goodness to us.

What's the secret meaning?

God wanted his chosen people to be
happy, that Jesus had come. But the
leaders didn't want to welcome him. So
the invitation was opened up to the rest
of the world like us. If we accept God's
invitation, we must be willing to want a
new life, which is given to us.

PROPER 24

Sunday between 16 and 22 October inclusive

Thought for the day

All leaders and rulers are subject to the ultimate authority and power of God, the living truth.

Readings

Isaiah 45:1-7
Psalm 96:1-9 (10-13)
1 Thessalonians 1:1-10
Matthew 22:15-22

Aim

To look at Jesus' teaching about giving to God what is God's and to Caesar what is Caesar's.

Starter

Price tags. Give out a selection of play money to each small group of children, and have some objects for them to 'buy'. Then call out a price tag: 'Here's a pair of scissors and it costs twenty pence.' The first group to come up with the exact money gets the pair of scissors. The group with most items bought is the winner.

Teaching

If you have any old or foreign coins, bring them along and pass them around, and also show the children pictures of Roman coins from library books. Draw their attention to the pictures on the coins. Who are the pictures of and why are they there?

Remind the children of how the Pharisees were becoming more and more keen to get rid of Jesus, and how they tried to catch him out with a cunning plan. In order to understand the trap, they will need to know something about the Romans. Using the books, tell them how the Roman empire covered lots of countries. The Romans would fight their way into a country and take it over, ruling over the people there. They needed money to build the roads and market places, the aqueducts to carry water and the public baths. Where did the money come from? All the people in the countries the Romans ruled over had to pay tax. Do you think they were happy to pay tax to the people who had taken over their country? No, they weren't. In fact they hated it!

Now that you know this, you will see what a clever trap was set to catch Jesus out. The Pharisees went up to Jesus with the crowds all around him and asked him a question. First they buttered him up. 'We know you are a good person,' they said, 'and you always tell the truth, even if it isn't what people want to hear.' (That's what had happened to them, wasn't it!) Then came the question (show this so they can all join in with asking it): 'Is it right to pay tax to Caesar or not?'

Now that was a tricky question. If Jesus said, 'Yes, it's right to pay tax to the Romans', what would the people who hated the Romans think? (They might think Jesus was sucking up to the Romans and not standing up for his own country.) And if Jesus said, 'No, it isn't right to pay tax to the Romans', what would the Romans do? (They would get him into big, big trouble.)

So what did Jesus do? He knew it was a trap. He asked to borrow a coin (pick one up) and he showed it to the people. 'Whose picture is on this coin?' asked Jesus. 'Caesar's,' they answered. Then Jesus said this: 'Then give to Caesar what belongs to Caesar and give to God what belongs to God.' (Have these words written out and all join in saying them.)

Clever, wasn't it? The Pharisees had set out to teach Jesus a lesson and trick him, but Jesus ends up teaching *them* and challenging them yet again to give God the honour he deserves.

Praying

Great is the Lord who has made heaven and earth.
He is our God and we are his people.
Lord God of earth and heaven,
we worship and adore you.

Activities

The children can make rubbings of some of the coins brought in, and use the world picture to make a car hanging. They will need to mount it on thin card, punch a hole in the top and have thread provided.

Notes

To pray this week

Great is the Lord
who has made heaven and earth.
He is our God
and we are his people.
Lord God of earth and heaven,
we worship and adore you.

How to make a 'God's World' car hanging

1. Colour both sides of the world

2. Stick them on each side of thin card

3. Punch a hole and thread string

2

what belongs 2

and 2

what belongs 2

give Caesar

GOD

IT'S GOD'S WORLD!

WHOSE WORLD?

Coin rubbings here

Proper 25

Sunday between 23 and 29 October inclusive

Thought for the day

We are to love God with our whole being, and love others as much as we love ourselves.

Readings

Leviticus 19:1-2,15-18
Psalm 1
1 Thessalonians 2:1-8
Matthew 22:34-46

Aim

To know the summary of the law.

Starter

Tape some lengths of wool to the floor, criss-crossing the circle where you are all sitting. Choose four or five people to cross the circle at the same time, walking along the lines. The rule to avoid collisions is that whenever you meet someone else, both of you get off the line, swap positions and carry on. Point out how useful the rule was; keeping it made life easier and better for everyone.

Teaching

You will need a full sheet of blue sugar paper as the background, yellowy green hills, a blue river, a brown trunk and branches, green foliage and red and yellow fruit. As you talk, gradually the picture is built up, sticking one layer over another. The completed picture should look something like this:

In the countries where lots of rain falls all the year round, the trees have plenty to drink, so their leaves grow well and stay green in the summer. The tree grows lots of juicy fruit. In places where there isn't much rain at all, like this picture, the grass gets yellowy and dies in the heat of the sun. The trees can't survive either. *But,* suppose there is a river flowing through the dry grass (stick it on) and suppose a tree grows up right beside the river (put on the trunk and branches). The roots of this tree can drink up the water from the river, so this tree grows lovely green leaves (put on the foliage) and they stay green. The tree beside the water can grow so well that it starts to have fruit – lots of fruit (stick on the fruits). Even when there are times when it doesn't rain, this tree beside the water is going to be fine, and have lots of fruit for the people and animals and birds to eat.

In the Bible, we are told how to live in the very best way, like trees planted beside streams of water. The Bible tells us that the river we need to live by is this:

To love God, and to love one another. (Write this in on the river of the picture.)

Live by this, and we'll grow and live strong and tall, with lots of good fruit in our life. Read the summary of the law, now that they know its outline.

Praying

Help us, Lord, to keep your law,
loving you with all we are,
loving other people too,
that's what we will try to do.

Activities

Sing this summary of the law to the tune of *London's burning*, in a round with actions.

You shall love the
  (*hands on heart*)
Lord your God with
  (*arms raised*)
all your heart and
  (*hands on heart*)
all your mind and
  (*hands hold head*)
all your strength! All your strength!
  (*show muscles in arms*)
And love your neighbour,
  (*arm round neighbour on one side*)
and love your neighbour.
  (*arm round neighbour on other side*)

Provide the children with the different shapes of coloured paper as shown on the sheet so they can make their own collage of the tree planted beside the water, with the summary of the law written on the river.

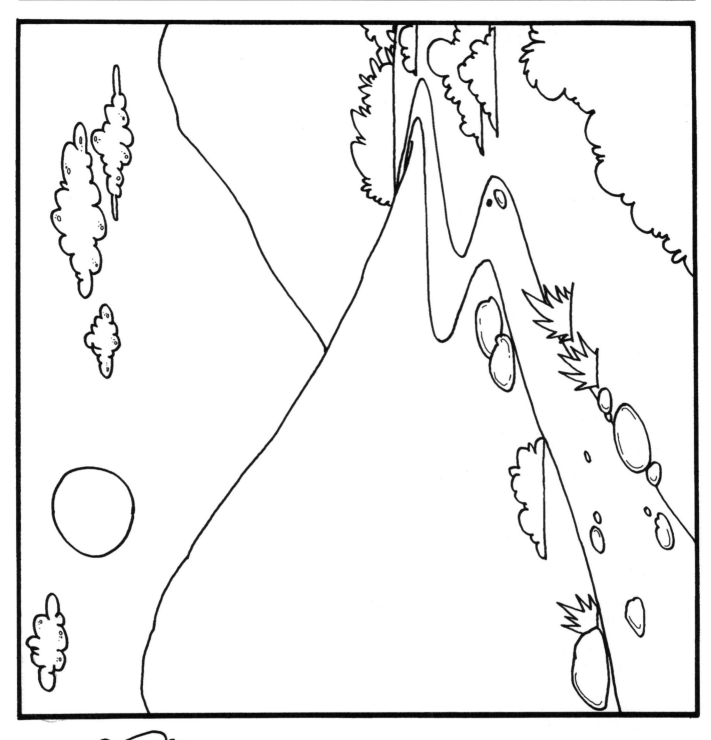

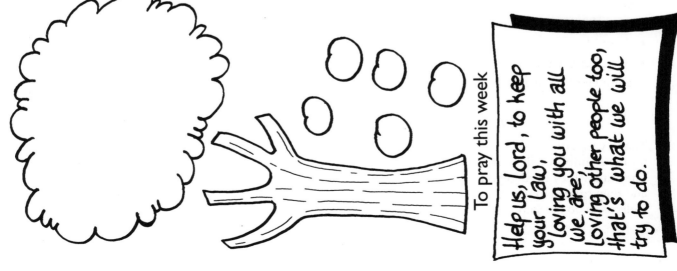

To pray this week

Help us, Lord, to keep your Law, loving you with all we are; loving other people too, that's what we will try to do.

ALL SAINTS' DAY

Sunday between 30 October and 5 November inclusive

Thought for the day

Lives that have shone with God's love on earth are filled with joy as they see their Lord face to face.

Readings

Revelation 7:9-17
Psalm 34:1-10
1 John 3:1-3
Matthew 5:1-12

Aim

To celebrate All Saints' Day, looking at the example of some of the saints.

Starter

Get in an 'expert' to help everyone learn to juggle. Give out rolled socks for this. If you have no jugglers to draw on, just pick some other expert, such as a cat's-cradle person, fitness trainer, Irish dancer or cartoonist. Looking at their example helps the rest of us get the hang of whatever we are trying.

Teaching

When we looked at the example of someone who had been practising for a long time, it helped us pick up the skill. Today is the day we celebrate a festival – all the saints who have been God's good friends down through the centuries, and now live in heaven, happy for ever in God's company. We thank God for their lives and their example to us.

They all started off as ordinary people and any of us could be saints. All it takes is to realise that we need God, and to walk with him closely through our lives. Let's look at where that took some of God's friends. Either draw as you talk, or have different children to be the saint in question.

- Saint Alban (a Roman soldier)
- Saint Margaret of Scotland (a queen)
- Saint Benedict (a monk)
- Saint Helena (an elderly lady)

Praying

Thank you, Lord God,
for the example of all your saints.
They knew they needed you
and they trusted in you.
Help us to do the same.

Activities

On the sheet there is an illustration to trace, so the children will need tracing paper (or greaseproof paper) and paper clips. There is also a saintly wordsearch.

Notes

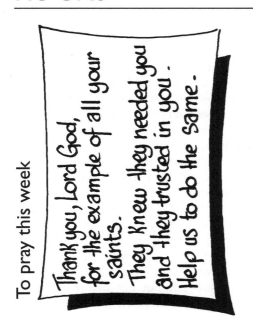

To pray this week

Thank you, Lord God, for the example of all your saints.
They knew they needed you and they trusted in you.
Help us to do the same.

R	W	N	J	B	D	G	T	F	B
Y	E	L	B	M	U	H	U	L	E
M	A	R	G	A	R	E	T	O	N
K	P	L	P	B	I	L	S	V	E
B	M	O	B	R	K	E	H	I	D
A	G	E	N	A	I	N	E	N	I
C	F	A	J	V	N	A	R	G	C
I	M	V	L	E	D	C	Z	H	T

MARGARET ALBAN HELENA
BENEDICT LOVING HUMBLE
BRAVE KIND

Trace the saints and colour them. Hold them up to the light.

Saint Margaret of Scotland

She was a Queen, and spent lots of time with God which made her a loving, generous person. She organised food and help for the poor, and brought happiness to many lives by her loving nature.

Saint Alban

He was a Roman soldier and hid a priest from persecution. The priest's example made him want to be a Christian and he swapped clothes so the priest could escape. Alban was taken and killed.

Saint Helena

She was over 60 years old when she became a Christian, but made up for that by the enthusiastic way she lived out her new faith. She overflowed with love and generosity, helped the poor and looked after prisoners.

Saint Benedict

He was an abbot at a monastery and worked out a rule of life for monks that was well balanced, with time given to prayer, reading and work with their hands.

God's light shines through their lives.

FOURTH SUNDAY BEFORE ADVENT

Sunday between 30 October and 5 November inclusive*

* For use if the Feast of All Saints was celebrated on 1 November and alternative propers are needed.

Thought for the day

With God's light and truth to guide us, we shall be brought safely through to the end of time.

Readings

Micah 3:5-12
Psalm 43
1 Thessalonians 2:9-13
Matthew 24:1-14

Aim

To know that Jesus' foretelling of the destruction of Jerusalem happened.

Starter

In teams they can try something which takes great care and concentration to the end of a course, such as carrying a very full bowl of water without spilling a drop, or walking with a couple of books on their heads.

Teaching

Point out how they had to keep concentrating carefully right to the end of the course in that activity. Today we hear some warnings about difficult times, but Jesus tells us that whoever perseveres to the end will be saved.

Show a picture of the temple. Explain how Jesus had been in the temple at the holy city of Jerusalem, and he was very sad, because he knew that, before many years, the city and the temple would be destroyed; the people had not listened to all the warnings they had been given, and mostly they hadn't recognised Jesus as the promised Messiah, or Christ. As he left the temple for the last time, Jesus told his friends that it would soon be nothing but a pile of rubble. They were very shocked, and they all walked on in silence for a bit. Then they said, 'Jesus, did you really mean that about the temple being a pile of rubble? We're worried – can you tell us when and how it's going to happen?'

So Jesus told them. (Give out items for the sound effects.) He told them that there would soon be lots of wars that would involve the Jewish people (clash of metal). There would be famines and plagues, so that many people would not have anything to eat,

and would die from hunger and illness (sound of crying). There would be terrible earthquakes all over the area (rattle cardboard sheets), and there would be false teachers, trying to lead people astray (I'm right, listen to me! No, listen to ME!). Jesus told them not to be flustered or panic in all this, because another thing that would happen was that the Gospel would be taught all over the place (God has sent his Son, Jesus, to save us and set us free!).

After all these things have happened, said Jesus, Jerusalem, the holy city, will be destroyed (crashing and banging). And that is what happened. Use a length of string as a time-line, with the words 'Jesus born' hung at one end and 'Today' at the other. Hang 'AD 70' at the appropriate place, and tell them that in AD 70 Jerusalem was taken by the Romans and destroyed. But not before all those other things had happened, just as Jesus had said.

If you have time you can run through them again, with the sound effects.

Praying

Dear Jesus,
it must have made you very sad
to know Jerusalem would be destroyed.
Why do we never listen to your warnings?
Why do we never hear?
Next time you warn us to guide us,
help us listen and take notice.

Activities

The sheet is divided into two so that one half is turned into a strip book with pop-up flaps, which are cut from the other section. They are helped to see that Jesus keeps with us all the time, both in the bad and the good.

<table>
<tr><td>

Notes

</td></tr>
</table>

To pray this week

Dear Jesus,
it must have made you very sad
to know Jerusalem would be
destroyed.
Why do we never listen to
your warnings?
Why do we never hear?
Next time you warn us to
guide us,
help us listen and take
notice.

THIRD SUNDAY BEFORE ADVENT

Sunday between 6 and 12 November inclusive

Thought for the day

We need to keep ourselves awake and prepared so that the Day of the Lord does not come to us as darkness rather than light.

Readings

Amos 5:18-24 or Wisdom of Solomon 6:12-16
Psalm 70 or Wisdom of Solomon 6:17-20
1 Thessalonians 4:13-18
Matthew 25:1-13

Aim

To know the parable of the unprepared bridesmaids and its meaning.

Starter

As they come in, the children can make torches by fixing shiny red flames on to sticks with rubber bands or sticky tape.

Teaching

Jesus was telling his friends about the future, and what would happen at the end of the world when he would come back in glory. He told this parable to help them understand. It's set at a wedding. If any of them have been bridesmaids or page-boys they will remember that there's a lot of waiting around to do at weddings, and the wedding in Jesus' story was just the same. Explain how in Jesus' time, the bride and groom would go to the bridegroom's house, and then come out in the evening for the party. All the bridesmaids would wait around near the bridegroom's house until they came out, so they could light the bride and groom's way to where the wedding feast was held.

The torches they carried were like ours – sticks with flames on the top. They soaked some material in oil and tied it on to a stick before lighting it, so they needed to have spare oil with them, ready for when the oil was used up.

In Jesus' story there were ten bridesmaids waiting for the bridegroom. Five had plenty of oil for their lamps and five hadn't been keeping themselves ready. When eventually the bridegroom was ready to go, the five unprepared bridesmaids panicked. 'Give us some of your oil!' they said. 'Ours is running out!' But the other five couldn't give their oil. If they had done that there wouldn't have been enough light from any of the lamps, so they sent the unprepared bridesmaids to buy some more oil.

By the time they got back, the bride and bridegroom had been led through the night by the lamps of the other five bridesmaids, and the whole wedding party had gone in to the feast. The five unprepared bridesmaids weren't recognised when they hammered on the door, so they missed out on the party, all because they hadn't kept their oil supplies at the ready.

Jesus said to his hearers, 'So you keep awake and keep prepared, because you don't know when the bridegroom will be returning, and if you aren't ready, you'll find yourselves shut out of the celebrations on the last day.'

He was talking about the time when he will return in all the glory of God at the end of time. And we all need to keep our lamps topped up with oil ready for that.

Praying

Give me oil in my lamp, keep me burning,
give me oil in my lamp, I pray,
give me oil in my lamp, keep me burning,
keep me burning to the break of day.

Activities

On the worksheet there are instructions for making jam-jar lanterns. Each child will need a nightlight, a jar, some garden wire and some string. There is also a waiting activity using a clock face.

Notes

IS IT TIME YET?

Draw the times on the clocks

Grandma and Grandpa are coming at 7 o'clock.

But we got to the station half an hour early. What time is that?

It's 5 o'clock and I'm hungry.

But dinner isn't until 6 o'clock. How long do I have to wait?

The news starts at 1 o'clock

and finishes at 1.45.

How long does it go on for?

MAKE A LANTERN

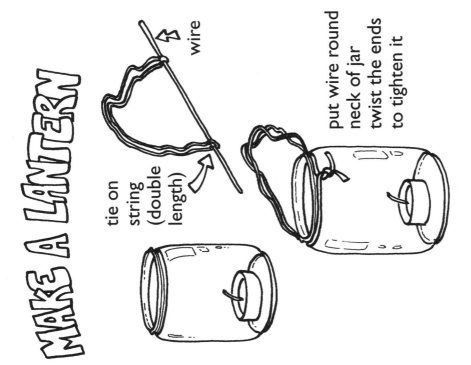

tie on string (double length)

wire

put wire round neck of jar twist the ends to tighten it

To pray this week

Give me oil in my lamp,
keep me burning,
give me oil in my lamp, I pray,
give me oil in my lamp,
keep me burning
keep me burning to the
break of day.

Second Sunday before Advent

Sunday between 13 and 19 November inclusive

Thought for the day

The Day of the Lord will hold terror for the wicked and unprepared, but rejoicing for those living in God's light.

Readings

Zephaniah 1:7, 12-18
Psalm 90:1-8 (9-11), 12
1 Thessalonians 5:1-11
Matthew 25:14-30

Aim

To know the parable of the talents and its meaning.

Starter

I am the music man, I come from down your way. There are lots of instruments the music man can play, which are 'played' by everyone in this song.

Teaching

Point out how talented the music man was in that song, able to play lots of different instruments. Today we are going to look at the gifts we have been given, and how God hopes we will enjoy them and make the most of them. Talk about the sort of gifts God gives us, such as being good at particular sports or skills, being thoughtful and kind, making people feel comfortable, helping them when they're ill, using money wisely, being able to work out answers to tricky problems, listening well, leading, or helping people make up after an argument. Some of us are given the happiness and security of a loving home, and others are given the gift of being cheerful even when life is difficult for us. All these things can be used to help the world.

Go round the group in circle time, with everyone saying, 'I'm glad God made me good at . . .'

Jesus told a parable about being responsible about our gifts, and using them, rather than hiding them away and ignoring them. As they will see, God expects us to make good use of whatever we are given.

Give out a copy of the script in the Appendix on page 135, to four people, who can act it out.

Praying

Lord God,
thank you for giving us gifts and talents.
Help us to enjoy them and use them well
for the good of the world.

Activities

There are instructions on the sheet for making some wrapping-paper, and the children will need plain coloured paper and an assortment of biscuit cutters to print with. There is also a wordsearch to reinforce the teaching of the parable, and a quiz to help them with the meaning of it.

Notes

To pray this week

Lord God,
thank you for giving us
gifts and talents.
Help us to enjoy them
and use them well
for the good of the world.

WHO'S WHO?

The man in the story is

and we are the ___ gives us ___

and wants us to use them wisely.

___ does not want us to

waste the ___ we are given.

GOD   Servants   gifts

K	I	N	G	D	O	M	O	T	A
R	A	I	H	E	A	V	E	N	C
S	O	N	F	A	V	E	D	N	C
E	N	Z	T	F	O	U	R	I	H
R	E	T	U	R	N	E	D	D	I
V	L	Y	S	S	M	E	R	A	D
A	O	C	E	T	O	N	E	Y	D
N	H	B	D	E	N	F	I	V	E
T	W	O	E	R	E	Z	I	B	N
S	A	N	G	R	Y	I	T	E	N

The **KINGDOM** of **HEAVEN** is like a man going away and leaving his **SERVANTS** to look after his things. He worked out how much each servant could cope with. To one he gave **FIVE** bags of **MONEY**, to another **TWO**, and to another **ONE**. When he **RETURNED**, he asked the servants to bring the money they had made. The first had made **TEN**, the second **FOUR**. But the third had just **HIDDEN** the money, and not **USED** it. The man was disappointed and **ANGRY** for not using his **GIFT**.

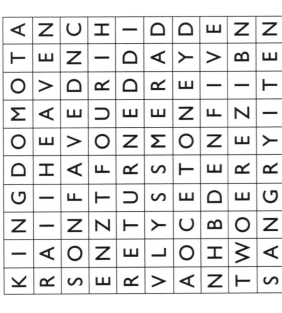

WRAP UP!

Make some wrapping paper and give someone a present. You will need

a sheet of coloured paper

thick paint and a brush or sponge

biscuit cutters

BLUE   RED

What you do

1. Fold the paper into squares

2. Print a shape in each square

CHRIST THE KING

Sunday between 20 and 26 November inclusive

Thought for the day

In total humility, at one with the least of his people, Jesus, the Messiah or Christ, reigns as King, with full authority and honour for eternity.

Readings

Ezekiel 34:11-16, 20-24
Psalm 95:1-7a
Ephesians 1:15-23
Matthew 25:31-46

Aim

To know the parable of the sheep and goats, and its meaning.

Starter

In teams the children pass a crown from head to head down the line, and the person at the end runs up to the front to start again. The first team to get back to the starting order wins.

Teaching

Jesus is like a Shepherd King, who looks after us all as his sheep, and searches for us when we are lost. Although he is King of the whole world and all time and space, he is always looking after our needs, more like a servant. Today we celebrate Christ as the humble King he is, full of glory but also full of love.

If we are going to be his people, we will act like him in our lives, and that is how he will recognise us as his people. Every time we do something kind or loving, or help someone, we are actually serving our King Jesus. Every time we are unkind and thoughtless, and don't notice that someone needs our help we are turning ourselves away from our King.

Jesus told one of his stories to help us understand. Place some carpet tiles, sheets or towels on the floor as the background for the story, and use cut-out pictures such as those shown on the sheet. You will need about twelve people. Move the pictures around on the background as you tell the story.

Jesus is talking about all the people standing before the throne of heaven who have not known him or been told about him during their lifetime. He says that the king is standing there and the people all stand in front of him. Just like a shepherd sorts out his sheep and goats he'll look at the people and put them into two groups, one on his right and the other on his left. To the ones on his right he will say, 'Welcome to my kingdom! I can see from your lives that you belong to my kingdom of love. When you were alive, you gave me food when I was hungry, drink when I was thirsty, you welcomed me when I was a stranger, you gave me clothes when I needed them, and you visited me and helped me when I was ill and in prison.'

Very puzzled, the people looked at each other and at the king. (Show the question mark over them.) 'We don't remember doing those things to you,' they said, 'When did we help you like that?'

The king explained to them that whenever they had done any of those kind things to anyone, they had been doing it to him. Their kind way of living showed, and that's how he could tell they were members of his kingdom of love.

Then he turned to the other group. 'I can see that you don't belong to my kingdom,' said the king. 'The way you lived your life shows up now. I was hungry but you never fed me, I was thirsty but you never gave me a drink. When I was a stranger you never invited me in, and when I needed clothes you didn't give me any. When I was ill and in prison you never came to visit me.'

The people were very surprised. (Show the question mark again.) 'We didn't do any harm in our life,' they protested. 'And we don't know what you mean – we don't even know you; when did we not help you?' The king looked at them sadly. 'I was there when you ignored the needs of those all around you and you just got on with your own lives without even noticing their pain and needs. When you failed to do good to those around you, you were failing to do good to me. That's how I can tell you don't belong in this kingdom of love. So you'll have to leave.'

And those people were sent away. Suddenly they realised that there is more to good living than just not hurting people. Good living is noticing needs and caring for them.

Praying

O Jesus, our King and our friend,
help us to live as your people,
aware of others' needs and ready to help.

Activities

Have the letters of 'Christ the Servant King' drawn on separate sheets of paper and let the children colour them all in, so they can be strung on to a length of wool and displayed in church. On the sheet is a pop-up card to make.

Glue flap here

Glue flap here

fold

Colour these in,
stick on the crown to make
a pop-up card

Read 'The Last Battle' by C. S. Lewis.
Especially, Chapter 15 – Further up and further in.

To pray this week

O Jesus, our king and friend,
help us to live as your people,
aware of others' needs
and ready to help.

stick to card

CHRIST IS OUR KING

fold

Stick to card

APPENDIX

Dem bones

Dem bones, dem bones, dem dry bones, dem

bones, dem bones, dem dry bones, dem bones, dem bones, dem dry bones, now

2nd time to

hear the word of the Lord. E – ze – kiel con–nec–ted dem dry bones, E –

ze – kiel con–nec–ted dem dry bones, E – ze – kiel con–nec–ted dem dry bones, now

hear the word of the Lord. 1. The toe bone con–nec–ted to the foot bone, the
(10.) neck bone con–nec–ted to the head bone, now

2. the foot bone connected to the ankle bone,
3. the ankle bone connected to the leg bone,
4. the leg bone connected to the knee bone,
5. the knee bone connected to the thigh bone,

6. the thigh bone connected to the hip bone,
7. the hip bone connected to the back bone,
8. the back bone connected to the shoulder bone,
9. the shoulder bone connected to the neck bone, the

Text: Spiritual
Music: Spiritual arr. Donald Thomson

Leader Excuse me, but we've heard something rather unusual happened at the wedding today. Do you know anything about it?

S 1 We certainly do! I've been a servant with this family for twenty years and I've never known anything like it.

Leader What happened, exactly?

S 2 It was really embarrassing because we ran out of wine! I don't know how that happened, but the family were very worried about it. I mean – you just *don't* run out of wine for your guests at a wedding, do you now?

Leader I suppose not. What did you do about it?

S 1 Well, one of the guests . . .

S 2 Mary, her name is. She's always very kind to us . . .

S 1 Yes, Mary overheard us panicking about the wine, and she beckoned us over.

S 2 She talked quietly so no one else would hear . . .

S 1 . . . and she pointed to her son, Jesus, who was also a guest.

S 2 He's nice, too. Always chats to you as if you're a real person instead of just a servant.

S 1 Well, anyway, Mary said, 'Do whatever he tells you.'

Leader 'Do whatever he tells you'?

S 1 Yes, that's right. So I went over to Jesus, thinking perhaps he knew where I could get some more wine real quick, before anyone had noticed I was missing.

Leader And what did he tell you?

S 2 He told us to fill the water jars with water.

Leader But I thought it was wine you were short of, not water?

S 1 Exactly! I must admit I thought it sounded an odd thing to do, but there was something about Jesus that made me sure I could trust him, and that he knew what he was talking about.

S 2 Yes, and his mother obviously reckoned we could trust him.

S 1 Yes. So we did what he said, and filled those big water jars right up to the brim. They're heavy when they're full.

Leader Then what?

S 2 Well, then he told us to pour out some for the most important guest.

Leader What – pour out water? Surely that would be an insult when he was expecting wine?

S 1 Well, the strange thing is, I felt sure it wouldn't be water when I poured it out – and it wasn't!

Leader What do you mean – it wasn't?

S 1 I mean that as I poured it out it was the most delicious looking wine I had ever seen.

S 2 It smelt really good, too.

Leader What did it taste like?

S 1 The guest took a few sips and started going on about how excellent it was.

S 2 Yes, he was congratulating the host for keeping the best wine until now!

Leader Did you tell them what had happened?

S 1 No, Mary and Jesus didn't want us to make a fuss. They just wanted to help us out, and show us how God wants to look after us.

Leader So how had he done it, do you think? Was it a trick?

S 2 I've been thinking about that. And, you know, the rain falls every year and gets turned into the grape juice which gets turned into wine, so in a way, water is always getting turned into wine.

Leader Yes, I suppose that's quite a miracle, isn't it? We tend to take it all for granted.

S 1 So perhaps Jesus was making us look at all God's loving kindness in a new way. It certainly made me remember how great God is.

S 2 Come on, let's get a move on with this washing-up. They say Jesus is going to be talking in the next village tonight, and we want to go and hear what he has to say.

Leader I'll let you get on then. Thanks for your time. Goodbye.

Leader Ah, good morning. You are Simon Peter, I believe.

Peter Yes, that's right. Nice of you to invite me to your church! Hello, children. Good to meet you!

Leader Peter, we wanted to ask you about what happened when Jesus took you up that high mountain in Galilee.

Peter Oh my goodness, I'll never forget that day, and that's for sure. He took three of us, you know – me and James and John – and I remember I got very hot and puffed out on the way up. I wasn't as young and fit as the others!

Leader What happened when you got to the top?

Peter Well, we three sat down for a rest and Jesus stood up, praying. He often used to go off on his own to pray, but this time we could see him. He wasn't just going through the words, he was deep in conversation with God. And then it happened.

Leader What happened?

Peter Well, although I saw it with my own eyes, it's quite difficult to describe. It was as if he was so much part of God as he prayed that he started to look . . . different.

Leader Different? How do you mean? Did he start changing shape or something?

Peter No, his whole face and clothes and everything seemed to be full of light, as if he was shining.

Leader Perhaps the sun was shining on him?

Peter Oh no, it wasn't like that. I've seen the sun shining on people lots of times. This lightness was as if it was all part of him. To tell you the truth, I felt a bit frightened. There was God present in all his glory and I was watching it happen! And there's something else.

Leader What?

Peter Jesus wasn't on his own.

Leader Not on his own? What on earth do you mean?

Peter Well, he wasn't only talking with God; he was talking with two other people – one was Moses. He's our wonderful leader who led us out of Egypt where we were slaves and gave us God's Law. Have you heard of the ten commandments? And the other person was our well-loved prophet Elijah. They were all talking together!

Leader Are you saying they were ghosts?

Peter No, they didn't seem to be ghosts exactly. It was more that we were outside the usual time and place rules because we were being allowed a peep into God's eternity and his glory.

Leader How amazing! Did you hear anything?

Peter We certainly did! We actually heard God's voice.

Leader How do you mean?

Peter Well, there was this bright cloud which kind of settled on us all, and God was speaking to us from it. Now I can't really tell you what it sounded like. I just know that when we heard God speaking to us it was so powerful that our legs turned to jelly and we fell on the ground – it was all too big for our bodies to cope with, I suppose.

Leader What did the voice say?

Peter It said, 'This is my beloved Son, who I'm well pleased with. Make sure you listen to him.' God was telling us that Jesus had God's authority, and I think we all realised then that he was much more than the wonderful friend and teacher we loved so much.

Leader Well, Peter, what an incredible experience! It's good to talk to someone who was actually there and saw it all. Thank you. Is there anything you'd like to tell us while you're here?

Peter Yes, there is. I'd like to tell you all what God told us and showed us on that mountain: Jesus really is God's Son, he has God's full authority, and you really do need to listen and take notice of what he says. We're talking about more than lifetimes here – we're talking about full life that never ends but lasts for ever.

Leader Thank you, Peter. We're gradually getting to know Jesus here, and we're amazed at the love he has for us. We'll certainly take your advice and listen out to what he says. Goodbye, and thanks again for coming.

Script for Proper 19

Narrator	In this story there is Mr Boss the master . . .
Mr Boss	Hello there!
Narrator	Servant Sam . . .
Servant Sam	Hi!
Narrator	. . . and Servant Ben.
Servant Ben	Good morning!
Narrator	Servant Sam had borrowed loads and loads of money from Mr Boss and one day Mr Boss called him in and demanded that the money should be paid.
Mr Boss	You owe me millions and I want my money back NOW! If you can't pay me, then you and your wife and children will have to be sold.
Servant Sam	Oh, Mr Boss! I haven't got the money to give you yet. Please, please, just give me time and I will pay it all.
Narrator	Mr Boss felt sorry for Servant Sam so he let him off.
Mr Boss	OK, Sam. I will let you off. It is a lot of money but you are free. You do not have to pay it.
Servant Sam	You mean I will never have to pay it?
Mr Boss	Never.
Servant Sam	Oh, thank you, thank you, Mr Boss! You are so kind. Yippee – I'm free!
Narrator	Servant Sam was very grateful and very happy. But later on he met Servant Ben who owed him a little money, and he got hold of Ben round the neck and shouted at him to give the money back.
Servant Sam	Come on, Ben, hand over my money. Hand it over NOW! I want it back!
Servant Ben	Oh, Sam, it's only a little bit of money, but I haven't got it to give you. Please give me time and I will pay it all.
Narrator	But Servant Sam wouldn't listen. He had Ben thrown into prison.
Servant Sam	Off to prison with you!
Narrator	When the other servants told Mr Boss about it, he was very upset and very angry, and he went to find Servant Sam.
Mr Boss	Sam, how dare you do that to Ben! You owed me loads of money and I felt sorry for you and let you off. But you did not let Ben off at all. So now I will throw you into prison!
Narrator	Servant Sam was kept in prison until he had paid every last penny.

Script for Second Sunday before Advent

Owner	I have to go away for a long time. I will put my servants in charge until I get back. Servants, come here!
Servants	Yes, sir, what do you want?
Owner	I have to go away for a long time and I am going to put you in charge until I get back. Servant Jack, I am giving you five bags of money to look after. Look after it well for me.
Servant Jack	OK, I will.
Owner	Servant Molly, I am giving you two bags of money to look after. Look after it well for me.
Servant Molly	OK, I will.
Owner	Servant Luke, I am giving you one bag of money to look after. Look after it well for me.
Servant Luke	OK, I will.
Owner	Now I am off. Use that money well and see what you can do with it. I will see you later. Good bye.
Servants	Good bye!

Later

Owner	Here I am! Come on, servants. Let's see how you used the gifts I gave you.
Servant Jack	Here you are. You gave me five bags of money and I have worked to make it ten.
Owner	Well done, you good and faithful servant. I will reward you.
Servant Molly	Here you are. You gave me two bags of money and I have worked hard to make it four.
Owner	Well done, you good and faithful servant! I will reward you.
Servant Luke	Here you are. I haven't done anything with the bag of money you gave me. I just hid it. You can have it back again now.
Owner	Just one bag of money? You lazy servant! I put you in charge of that. You should have used it, not just hidden it. I will give this one bag of money to servant Jack. He made very good use of the gifts I gave him. Out of my sight, servant Luke!